A Pilot's Story

By John L. Gaston, Lt. Col. USAF Retired

With Leonard Gaston

ISBN-13:978-1515227632
ISBN-10:1515227634

This book is personally dedicated to the following

Friends who have helped my daughter and me to find and make a home. Rodney Cheek (ex-Air Force), Pat and Denis Benington (ex-Air Force), Jack Mills (there is no such thing as an *ex*-Green Beret), and so many others... you know who you are and I am endlessly grateful to you for your friendship and support.

My comrades of long ago in the Checkertail Clan. To members of the Checkertail organization; the proud memory of those men still lives because of you. And thank you dear friends of Lesina, Italy, for the monument you erected in memory of those who fought for the freedom of your people and ours. How much I appreciate the recognition you gave them.

Kathy Gaston. My daughter whose love and care for me have been an inspiration to me and all who know her.

Greg Gaston. Ph.D. Without his dedication and creativity this book would not have come about.

Vic Olsen. Close friend of Leonard's from the academic world. Brilliant Austrian-school economist. Stalwart Christian recently gone to be with The Lord Jesus Christ, and greatly missed by friends and family.

Jim Davis. the best friend Leonard ever had. Loyal, brave, and honorable. Devoted to his young family. He was lost on a mission defending his country.

Professional Acknowledgments

Brenda Van Niekerk
www.triomarketers.com
Brenda - Without your exceptional talent and personal care this book would have been impossible. You have our heartfelt thanks!

Laura Shinn
www.laurashinn@yolasite.com
Laura -Your artistic talent is the greatest. Thank you!

Author's Preface

From the time as a very small boy I saw an airplane fly overhead, I wanted to fly. I would build rough models out of old boards and later on flying models from balsa wood and tissue paper. My hard-working family encouraged this interest. I am indebted to my father and mother, to my older brother, and to my two older sisters, for the way they taught me duty and responsibility - not by words - but by example. Of the world's goods we had little, but we had something better, a close-knit, loving family.

I am grateful also to my high school teachers, some excellent flight instructors, and mentors who inspired me. Our high school superintendant, Martin Grantham, was an amazing man. Some fifty years later, at a high school reunion, he asked me about my older brother and sisters, and remembered each by name. My family had great respect for him and for our principal, Frank Harris, and others. R. E. Capsey was my science teacher and athletic coach. George Kronderis taught math and served as assistant coach. John Mathery, who taught vocational agriculture, was another exceptional teacher.

Of those comrades along the way who were an inspiration to me how can I possibly say enough? The men of the 325th Fighter Group: We fought together and many gave their lives in the service of their country. In this group, Vernon Bradeen, who shared what might be called our luxurious tent home with me and two other pilots. He was my best friend. The professionals of the 85th Air Transport Squadron: Their hazardous duties cost some their lives in long flights over the lonely Pacific.

The top flight men who maintained the aircraft I flew - two I can name: Clifton "Pat" Patterson my crew chief with the 325th and Red James, my assistant crew chief.

Perhaps the finest pilot I have ever known, Tommy Mayson. Certainly the most fun to fly with. One stormy, tumultuous evening in Colorado we had great fun demonstrating an aircraft his employer had for sale. The attorney we demonstrated it to was impressed with our skill (I think he was relieved to get back on the ground alive) but he didn't buy the airplane. And another pilot extraordinaire, Clinton Kearney.

What rich memories you have made possible. I owe you all so much.

As I sit here in the peaceful setting we currently enjoy, I often see deer out my window grazing quietly. After a career involving travel and flights across the country and much of the world, I feel I have come home. I look back and wonder how anyone could be so privileged as to have the experiences I have had, to do what I always wanted to do … to fly.

John Gaston

Table of Contents

Chapter One: It Began Here

The bright yellow cub sailed smoothly outward, outlined against the blue sky. The prop stopped, the nose pitched up in a perfect power off stall, the stable little aircraft dropped its nose evenly and recovered. It swooped down in a long, gentle glide, performed another power-off stall, recovered again, and landed smoothly on the rough surface. The gear caught and it nosed gently over. I hastened down the slope of the huge straw pile on our Kansas farm - left from a recent threshing of wheat and piled high to be used later for livestock bedding - and picked my model up from where it had landed. It was undamaged. I climbed back to the top of the stack, rewound the rubber band that would drive the propeller again for a few seconds, and released it to fly again.

I was probably in the fifth or sixth grade and I had wanted to fly since the first time, as a little boy, I had watched an airplane go by overhead, fascinated by the sight.

Years later, newscasts on the radio in our Kansas farm house, powered by an auto battery on the floor under its small table, brought us stories of war in Europe. Families around us began to worry that war would come to our country. In conversations between neighbors, they expressed concern that husbands, sons, and fathers would be called into the armed forces and sent off to fight on foreign soil.

The author's father in 1943

There was a lot of work to do on our farm, and my brother and I both worked to share the load with our hard-working father. It took all the money our parents could muster to make it possible for us to go to high school - a dozen miles away over sometimes impassible dirt roads. They rented a cramped apartment in a converted garage in Frankfort, Kansas, for us to live in one year. Other years, spaced out as we were, sometimes we drove the dirt roads, some years my sisters did house cleaning and prepared meals in return for room and board in town

My brothers, My Sisters, and I. Approximately 1939.

I had managed to earn enough money to pay for a correspondence course from which I learned some of the fundamentals of Aeronautics. I studied those lessons religiously.

The summer before my senior year my older brother and I worked on a railroad extra gang repairing damage to the Union Pacific caused by floods. I was only seventeen but told them I was eighteen. Brother Buck's skill at anything he turned his hand to was widely respected in our community and he had hired to drive a combine for harvests across the area that summer. But he hired on with the railroad and remained three weeks to be sure his little brother would be all right, and then resigned and drove combine throughout the wheat harvest.

The Big Blue River was notorious for flooding and that spring had done considerable damage. We ate our meals and slept in bunk cars with some of the roughest, toughest men you can imagine. I learned that most of these men - tough and hardened as they were - had good hearts, were intensely loyal to their friends, and lived by their own code of honor.

The money my brother and I earned that summer was enough to buy a used car, a 1936 Chevy, and give it to our father to replace the family car – an old Ford Model "A" which was on its last legs. That used Chevy was considered a marvelous car: we were told it had been driven only on paved roads and streets in Kansas City. It had never "plowed" – as farmers put it then – through the mud on unpaved dirt roads. My earnings also made it possible to actually get in the air when a barnstormer landed his Curtis Robin in a hay field two miles southeast of our farm. For a dollar from each of us the pilot took a friend and me for a brief but exhilarating ride. He took off, circled our nearby farmhouse, and landed.

A Curtiss Robin similar to the one in which my friend and I took a ride.

Another early barn-stormer. That's my Father in the foreground, wearing the hat.

When there was time, on a Sunday afternoon or by the light of a kerosene lamp at night during the week, when I wasn't studying, I built balsa and tissue paper airplane models. There was a tradition around our house, if a picture from my sister's box camera did not come out, and the film was clear, someone would say "Save it for John LeRoy". My sister would carefully put it aside for possible future use to make a windshield for one of my models.

I turned eighteen two weeks after graduating from high school and found a job working on a railroad "section gang" at Lillis, Kansas. That group was responsible for track maintenance over some fifteen or twenty miles (I do not recall exactly) of Union Pacific main line. The men in that crew were mostly of Irish descent, a hard-working, tough bunch of men. I worked hard right along beside them and they accepted me as one of them. One day we had been lifting track and driving spikes. I had learned the art of working in synchronization with another man as we alternately delivered blows to the head of the spikes with our large, two-handed spike driving hammers. We used a little motor car that ran on the rails to transport us to the work site. At quitting time I was helping to lift the car back on the track and as I started to straighten up, my back locked. Two of the men saw what had happened, alertly picked me up, still in a locked, bent over position, put me on the car, and back we rode to the section house.

Years later, when my mother's funeral procession had made its way to the old hilltop cemetery north of Frankfort, Kansas, a man came up to me and asked "John, is that your mother?" He knew me instantly. And I knew him. He was the foreman from that section gang. Retired from the railroad after a career of hard labor, he was now a grounds keeper in the cemetery, mowing the sparse grass and keeping weeds away from the grave sites. He said, and I will never forget his sincerity, "Don't worry John, I'll take care of her."

On November 27, 1942, five months after I turned 18, I enlisted as a private in the Army Air Corps. The United States, unprepared for war, was frantically building up its training and processing centers in order to throw more manpower into the conflict. In our well-worn 1936 Chevrolet sedan, I drove from our farm to Kansas City to enlist, and then to Fort Leavenworth to take the enlistment physical. I was then told, "Go home, and we will call you."

My father, mother, and little brother. Approximately 1944.

The call came in January to report back to Kansas City the first week in February. There I was put on a train with a number of other enlistees and sent to Jefferson barracks near St. Louis, Missouri. I remember that it was night, and the train's coaches were very old and very cold, as was Jefferson Barracks after we arrived. We were issued uniforms and assigned a tent in which to sleep. Each tent had wooden walls, a canvas top, and a small wood-burning stove in the center. We spend a great deal of our basic training time drilling and marching about in the snow. Our drill instructor was a much-disliked Army PFC, who carried a swagger stick and took apparent delight in bossing around a group of men who had the distinction of being earmarked for flying duty.

I don't remember exactly how long we stayed at "Pneumonia Gulch" as we called it, but it was too long. As best as I can remember, it was sometime in early March that a large group of recruits, with me among them, was marched to the train station for departure. There was one hurdle. Anyone found to be ill, and many of us were because of the bad living conditions, would be held over. I had such a bad case of laryngitis that I could not speak. When my name was called, I nudged the man next to me and he yelled, "Here!" I made it on the train and was off to Beloit College in Wisconsin for a short stay in what was called a College Training Detachment or CTD.

Whatever the officially stated purposes of the CTD's were, it appeared to most of us that they actually had two main objectives: they benefited the colleges whose enrollments had been cut in half by the removal of most of their male students, and they furnished a place to hold aviation recruits like cattle until they could be run through the training pipeline. My contingent ended up in a fine school however, where we were assigned to classes with math and physics heavily emphasized. Before leaving Jefferson Barracks we had been tested and, based on our test scores, assigned to five groups, 60 men to a group. Those who tested highest would spend the briefest time in the CTD and would be shipped out first.

It was a tribute to the teachers in my small Kansas high school, and to parents who put great stress on study, that I ended up in the first group. One of only a half dozen fresh high school graduates in that group, I was in over my head and would have sunk had it not been for the tutoring given to me by my three dormitory roommates. We were assigned four to a room and the other three were far better prepared for the academic race we were about to run.

Two were particularly helpful. One, Ken Dunaway, was a CPA. He survived the war and later worked for Chrysler Corporation for many years. The second, John Gaddis, was from Larned, Kansas. He was a graduate engineer and had come to the Army from a promising career at Pillsbury, the company to which he returned after the war. Our group of overachievers was dumped directly into junior and senior level courses that included spherical trigonometry, philosophy, and other subjects beyond my experience.

Of course physical training continued unabated. Beloit College had a highly respected swimming coach who was assigned the job of assuring that all of us could swim before we are allowed to proceed further in the aviation program. I can still remember him running up and down the side of the pool screaming in frustration at the two or three men who seemed incapable of ever passing the required test: swimming the length of the pool and back. I was one of that number. It was here, I believe, that the physical training we were put through every day, which followed years of hard work on the family farm and working on railroad track gangs paid off. I could not master the art of breathing and swimming at the same time, but I managed to pass the test by holding my breath, swimming underwater the length of the pool, coming up on the other end to take a breath, and swimming back, underwater. It wasn't according to the training syllabus, but it allowed me to pass the test.

The author and a friend at Beloit College in Wisconsin.

After a few short weeks in the CTD, the day came when our group was put on yet another train and away we went, this time to the Santa Anna, California, classification Center. Here there was more processing and there were more physical exams. (No laryngitis or fever this time!)

The author at Beloit College 1943

The author at Beloit College in early 1943, Age 18.

We were given a battery of tests to determine if we would have the opportunity to become pilots, bombardiers, or navigators. We all waited eagerly for the results. After two days the results were posted: you're this, you're that - and that was it. Then we were put in a human holding pattern until there was space for us in preflight school. It was now early June, and I was assigned to class 44-B.

The pressure to get more men into the training pipeline and the sheer numbers involved were highlighted by an otherwise insignificant item, uniforms. My older brother, after a stint in the Army Coast artillery, had been assigned to class 43-G. At that time, they had been given a cadet uniform somewhat different from regular Army attire. Only a few months later, would-be aviators were wearing standard Army olive drab to their nine weeks of preflight classes. My particular group, which it been rushed through CTD, was told on its arrival at Santa Anna that it would be designated class 44-BX and would have the honor of completing preflight training in three weeks instead of the customary nine. (They needed pilots for the war!)

It is worth noting here that Army Air Corps leaders went into World War II with an overly optimistic view of the efficacy of heavy aerial bombardment. I learned much later, upon reading Ira Eaker's book, *Air Force Spoken Here*, that initial losses of planes and flight crews were much heavier than expected, and the start of a large-scale air war over Europe had to be delayed until they could get more aircraft and more people into the pipeline to replace the projected severe losses.

But we knew little of this at the time. Most of us just wanted to get on with the business of learning to fly and helping to win the war. At the end of our three short weeks of preflight, those of us designated for pilot training were put on a train and sent to primary flying school at what had been the Ryan School of Aeronautics at Hemet, California, which was now called Ryan Field. There we were introduced to the PT-22. Some called it the "San Diego Messerschmitt". We called it the "Maytag Messerschmitt" after the one cylinder gasoline powered washing machines in widespread use at that time.

The PT-22 A beautiful little airplane. Photo courtesy of Jerry Bates

Primary training took about two months, and during this time we accumulated approximately 65 hours of flying time. I recall that I soloed after four hours and 50 minutes of flight instruction. I thought that my first instructor, Gordon Helm, did a super job. (In Hemet in 1984, I found his name in the telephone book and called his home, but was saddened to learn that a man who it done so much to get me ready for flying duty was no longer among us).

The young flyers who had successfully soloed were passed on to other instructors. My instructor, Fred Workman, had a unique "relaxation maneuver" to test the mettle of his charges. After they were thoroughly stressed-out from practicing aerial drills, he would roll the aircraft upside down and tell a student to do a coordination exercise. The student was then required to rock the aircraft from side to side with the ailerons while at the same time keeping the nose pointed constantly at a convenient mountain. Adding interest to the task was the fact that the PT - 22 had a float - type carburetor, so the engine quit almost immediately after the aircraft was rolled to an inverted position. Consequently, the student had to glide, upside down, hanging by his seatbelt, rocking the aircraft, and coordinating movement of the rudder to combat the yaw introduced by the ailerons. Fortunately, the prop was windmilling, so when the aircraft descended to the point where it had to be turned upright, the engine always started.

After finishing with the PT - 22, I was marched aboard yet another train, along with other survivors of primary training, and transported to the next hurdle that stood between us and the coveted silver wings awarded to those who completed pilot training. That hurdle was basic flight training at Merced Army Airfield at Merced, California.

At Merced, we were introduced to the BT-13. Most of us thought it was a huge aircraft. I had an additional reason to view it with some trepidation. Early in the war, many civilian flight instructors had been sent to a central instructors' school at Randolph Field where they completed a training program, were commissioned as second lieutenants, and designated "service pilots" who would instruct future combat pilots. At the airfield where we earlier had received 4 to 5 hours of familiarization flights in light planes while in the CTD, there had been one instructor who had gone to Randolph, seen the BT-13, pronounced it too much aircraft to fly, and passed up a commission. I was aware of this. Now I had to master this awesome aircraft.

The BT-13. Huge and imposing on the ramp. Photo courtesy of Jerry Bates.

The pressure on us mounted. I don't remember how long it took me to solo, but it was longer than had been necessary for the PT - 22. One incident from basic stands out in my memory - night flying. One afternoon, most of the cadets in our class were bussed out to an auxiliary field for our first night flying experience. Through the luck of the draw, I had the opportunity to fly out to the site. My instructor and I climbed into the BT-13 and arrived at the auxiliary field just before the sun was to go down. After my required three landings (it was by no means dark yet) he said, "OK - "You're checked out" and climbed out of the airplane. Normally I would have been sent out to orbit near the field until called in to turn the aircraft over to another student. However the aircraft I happened to be in was designated a spare, so I was told to simply stay in the pattern and shoot landings. "If we need the airplane, we will call you in." I took off, and as it got darker and darker I just continued to shoot landings. Midway through the training session all aircraft were called in, and I landed and parked the airplane. I figured that I wouldn't get to fly any more that night. However an announcement was made there was another spare aircraft. "Who would like to fly it?" I jumped at the chance to fly more and was told once again, "Just stay in the pattern and shoot landings. We will call you in if we need you." I took off before they could change their minds and continued to shoot landings, now in pitch darkness, for another two hours or more. Finally, all aircraft were ordered to land, concluding the scheduled training session.

Normally at that point the cadets would be loaded back on buses and instructors would fly the planes back to the main base. This time, however, an announcement was made that there were two spare aircraft, and a call was made for volunteers to fly them home. When asked, "How many landings do you have?" (three was the standard) I truthfully answered "Thirty four." "How did you get to do that?!" The officer in charge simply said, "OK. Go out and get in the aircraft and fly it back to the base." And so I had my first night cross-country, only a few hours after making my first night landing.

Soon after, along with other survivors of basic training, I was put on another train to head for Phoenix, Arizona. I left behind the now comfortable BT-13. Upon arrival, we were put on trucks (much like cattle again) and hauled to Williams field. We were designated as twin-engine fighter pilots, and looked forward eagerly to the day when we would fly P-38's. But more hurdles remained ahead and twists of fortune that would alter our futures.

By this time, the vagaries of processing had separated me from my friends from the brief days at Beloit College. Dunaway went to advanced flight training at Luke field, a single engine fighter school. I don't know where Geddis went.

Four or five students were assigned to each instructor. The first instructor my small group of would-be pilots encountered had less than a benevolent attitude toward his students. Within our small group he soon became known as "Reckless Red," a name that stuck with us long after we had forgotten his real name. It was generally believed that he thought he should be flying P -38s and not messing with students. I recall to this day his comment when he crawled out of our training aircraft, the AT-6, before I was to solo, "You go ahead and take it around. I'm going down to the meat wagon in case they have to come out and pick you up." The solo flight was uneventful.

We then went through ground school for the P-322, which was a P-38 with Allison engines and no turbo-superchargers. These had been built for the British and then the British didn't want them. Before being allowed to fly that aircraft however we received initial twin- engine flight training in the AT-9. After five hours in the "Curtis Rock" as we called it, we were scheduled to fly the P-322 for the rest of our advanced flight training.

The AT-6. Photo courtesy of Jerry Bates

The great day arrived when we were to check out in the beautiful P-38 look-alike. I was number three in line. Cadet number one broke the aircraft.

Day two arrived. I was number two in line. Cadet number one broke the aircraft.

On day three I was number one. While I was doing the walk around for my long-awaited flight in the P322, the public address system ordered all cadets to report to operations. I had just decided that I had not heard the announcement, because, after all, I was to fly almost immediately. Just then a nearby instructor bellowed, "Mister! Did you hear that?" I decided that I had heard it after all and reported to operations.

We were herded into a group and asked for volunteers for photo reconnaissance duty. I didn't volunteer. I wanted to fly and fight, and besides, I wanted more than anything else right then to get back to that beautiful bird waiting for me on the ramp outside. I was near the door and as I started to edge outside another announcement froze me in place, "Wait! The rest of you are hereby designated as single engine fighter pilots. You will finish your advanced training in the AT-6."

I did, and on February 8, 1944, was awarded the silver wings that came with the successful completion of an incredibly intense training program. After the entire ordeal was over I was told that, on the average approximately seven and a half men out of every one hundred who started the aviator training pipeline made it to commission flying status: two bombardier's, two and one half navigators and three pilots. Since that time I have seen other figures which indicated the passing rate was considerably higher, but the exact official figures, I do not know.)

Graduates then received a short leave to visit home. One man, who owned an old Ford V-8 with worn tires and no spare (local boards severely rationed the scarce supply of tires) announced that he was going to Denver and would take anyone who wanted to go along. Four of us started out and reached a bleak spot north of Socorro, New Mexico, when one of the tires blew. Two of us stayed with the car while the owner and one other man hitchhiked to town to try to talk the local ration board into an authorization to buy a new tire. Fortunately, we all had orders to report to distant points in short order and the board found that fact persuasive. The two returned with a replacement tire, and a spare, and the group continued on to Denver.

There, I bought a train ticket to Manhattan, Kansas, where my father and sister met me. We immediately set out for Lincoln, Nebraska, where my mother was waiting. My older brother, by now a copilot on a B-24, was staged there, scheduled to depart the next day to fly overseas. We spent the night talking together in the lobby of a Lincoln hotel, not knowing if we would see each other again in this life. Years later, after becoming a parent myself, I could more fully appreciate the way my mother and father must have felt that night as their sons prepared to go off to war.

Early next morning father, mother, sister, and I set out for home, our farmhouse in Northeast Kansas. Shortly after arriving there, we heard the noise of a four engine aircraft and ran outside to watch my brother's B-24 circle twice around the farmstead. It then flew away towards the southeast to start its long journey, first to South America, then across the South Atlantic to North Africa, and eventually to Italy.

After a few short days at home I was off to Dover, Delaware by way of Richmond,

Virginia. I had learned that I was to fly P-47s (a plane that only shortly before, as a future P-38 pilot, I had considered less than a first-class aircraft). But it was what I was assigned to, and it was what I would do. My first flight changed my mind, and I fell in love with the "Thunderbolt." But that first flight was an adventure.

The Awesome P-47. Photo courtesy of Jerry Bates

The pressure to pour more pilots into the combat theaters was relentless, and the transformation of new pilots into Thunderbolt drivers illustrated that fact. We were given one and a half days of ground school, where we learned about the aircraft's subsystems, and then a few minutes of "cockpit time." A P-47 was parked in a hangar with steps leading up to one side of the cockpit, and another set of steps leading down to the hangar floor from the other side. It was step up, and step down. Each of us climbed into the cockpit while an instructor squatted on the wing and ran through a quick description of the switches and controls, "This is this, and that is that." And then it was, "Next man!"

We were bussed to the operations shack and taken for a brief ride around the field in a BT-13. After all, it helps to know what the airfield you just left looks like from the air when you want to return. We then stood around and waited for whatever would happen next. I recall looking over the shoulders of three other pilots trying to read what seemed to be one of only two sets of P - 47 operating instructions available, trying to learn what I could. Then a major, J. W. Dixon, came in and commanded, "Gaston, get your chute." The conversation that followed lives vividly in my memory. "Where are we going?" "We're going to fly." "Fly what?" "The P-47." Then he asked: "Did you ever fly a P-47 before?" "No sir." "Did you ever fly a fighter?" "No sir." "Not even a P-40?" "No sir." (Most advanced single-engine students got some time in the P-40, but my small group, switched at the last minute from twin-engine duty, had only a few additional hours in the a AT-6.) "What have you flown?" "The AT-6 and the AT-9." "No sweat. It flies about like an A T-6." (All this time we're walking out to the aircraft.)

"How much cockpit time do you have in the P-47?" "About two minutes." (Silence for a little while) "Well, you probably don't know how to start the airplane." "No sir." "No sweat. I'll get in and start the airplane. You get up on the wing and watch." So he did, and I did, and the huge radial engines sat there turning at idle. "I'll tell you what I'll do. You stay there on the wing. I'll taxi it out away from the other airplanes." (The P-47, sitting on its conventional gear, had a huge engine nacelle that blocked the forward view of the taxiing pilot, and there was no point in letting this green young pilot damage more than one aircraft.)

He taxied it out and set the parking brake. I climbed into the cockpit, and he showed me how to buckle the shoulder harness (I had never worn one before). He then put a hand on my shoulder and asked, "Any questions?" (I didn't know enough about it to ask any questions). "Well, No sweat." "Just don't attempt any turns below a hundred and fifty indicated, and remember that you'll have to start your flare on landing just a little earlier than you did in the AT-6." "Go ahead and take it out for an hour so. When you feel comfortable, bring it back." In something that must have been like a state of shock I heard him say, "Good luck" and I was left with the airplane.

I taxied out to the run-up pad and went through the run-up procedure. I knew that something would have to be wrong. I shouldn't fly this airplane! The tower operator spoke brusquely, "You are cleared for takeoff." I ran through the engine run up procedure again. Everything checked out perfectly. The tower operator was well aware that this was checkout day, and he growled again, "You *are* cleared for takeoff." Not knowing what else to do, I slowly taxied the thunderbolt out and started down the runway.

The instructors had told us that the aircraft would fly itself off the runway at about 110 indicated. As I started to roll faster, I raised the tail so that I could see down the runway. (They hadn't bothered to tell us not to do that!) One ten went by, and then 130, and the airplane wasn't flying yet. But it was picking up speed fast, and the end of the runway was approaching at an alarming speed. At 150 I decided this bird had to know what it was built for and eased back on the stick. When it lifted off I raised the gear (no point in leaving it down if the aircraft decided to settle back and run off the end of the runway). But it did not settle back. When I increased the angle of attack at that speed, it left the ground in a most gratifying manner and showed that it did indeed know what it was built for.

Everything was going great. I began to relax just a bit and thought, "You know, this isn't half bad!" I adjusted to climb power and after gaining altitude, played around for a while. Soon an hour had passed, and it was time to go back. I was getting quite comfortable with the machine, which was handling nicely. I took it into the pattern and brought it down: Gear down. Flaps Set. "This is a piece of cake!" About that time, too late, I remembered I was supposed to flare a little sooner. They had told us that it was not possible to bounce the incredibly heavy P-47, but it was. It bounced once and then a second time. As it finally settled on the runway a voice from the tower gave a bronco rider's cheer, "Yipee!"

And that was my first flight in the Thunderbolt. It was a beautiful airplane that many pilots besides myself learned to love - a tough, dependable fighting machine. Although I then received more than 125 hours of training in the P-47, I was destined never to fly it in combat. Another twist of circumstances would send me to the 325th Fighter Group, the greatest fighter outfit in Europe, where I would fly the sleek P-51 Mustang.

Chapter Two:
The Checkertail Clan

Flight training in the U.S. Army Air Corps in World War II was a hurry-up process. I joined the Army in November 1942, six months after graduating from high school. The Army called me for induction the following February, as soon as a training slot opened up. I graduated from flight school with my silver wings 12 months later, in early February 1944. After three months of additional training in the P-47 "Thunderbolt", the airplane I expected to fly in combat, I found myself on an LST (Landing Ship Tank) on my way to war. I passed my 20th birthday on a convoy making its slow way across the stormy Atlantic.

In the first half of 1944 the pace of the Air War against Fortress Europe was increasing, as additional planes and crews reached the European theater. In the Mediterranean area, where I eventually found myself, allied forces had fought their way across North Africa, and our ground troops then invaded Italy. When they captured territory in southern Italy, aircraft from the 12th Air Force moved to bases there to support them by targeting German forces and transportation systems in northern Italy. The 15th Air Force, which I would eventually join, was dedicated primarily to targets deeper in Europe. As allied ground forces fought their way north, the 15th set up bases close behind the lines to shorten the journey to target. The base where I would end up was a bare 50 miles south of the bomb line.

Against this backdrop of accelerating air warfare, my class (44-B) completed flying training on 8 February 1944. After a short leave, I reported to a replacement training unit (RTU) at Dover, Delaware, where I had about 125 hours of training in the

P-47. Then I was sent to Richmond, Virginia, for assignment and further processing, and in turn to Camp Patrick Henry for final processing for overseas shipment. After a few days there, our small group of eager new fighter pilots was put on still another train and taken to a dockside embarkation point. It was there that the circuitous journey began that would eventually land me in Italy, a member of the 318th Fighter Squadron, 325th Fighter Group, the Checkertail Clan.

John Gaston Age 19

When our group of approximately 40 replacement pilots arrived at the embarkation point, the Dockmaster told us that the ship we were to board had departed the day before to take its place in a convoy that was being formed outside the harbor. The convoy, however, was not scheduled to depart until night. If we were interested, they said they would load our bags on a launch and take us out to locate the ship. We were all eager to go, so we loaded up and went outside the sub gates (which were open during the day but shut at nightfall to prevent German submarines of sneaking into the harbor) and started looking for the ship.

As we searched on that first day in June, 1944, late afternoon came, and the ship was nowhere to be found. The seaman running the launch made it clear that he had to head back to get inside the sub gates before they closed. We hailed an LST (Landing Ship Tank) and asked them if they had seen our ship. They had not, but there were three LSTs in their group and as far as they knew the convoy was all going the same place. If we wanted to split up into three groups they would take us. This was done. We bunked in spare bunks in the officers' cabins, about a dozen Army second lieutenants to each LST, most likely in better quarters than we would have had on the troop transport, if we could have found it.

An LST in port, loading troops.

The convoy pulled out on schedule. I was on the same LST as our troop commander, Capt. George T. Buck. Before we left Camp Patrick Henry he had been given a sealed package containing our special orders, which he was to open 24 hours after convoy departure. When the hour arrived, we all gathered around the table in the wardroom and watched as he opened the package. To our surprise, there were no special orders in the package, only a few pamphlets containing lectures on healthful living in the Middle East. We had no idea what our destination was, where we were supposed to go, or anything else. All we knew was that we were pointed in the right direction.

We asked the ship's captain what port we were going to. He either did not know or chose not to tell us.

We had the run of the ship including the chart room, and were able to determine that we appeared to be headed through the gates of Gibraltar to some place in the Mediterranean. At the convoy's rate of speed, which we estimated at about eight knots, that would take us about three weeks. We had in our small group two individuals who had some insight into what we called "cards." One had supposedly operated a pool hall before entering the Army. The other, it was rumored, had some experience running a game in the backroom of a saloon. They decided that, for entertainment, they would set up a game that would run approximately 3 weeks, with the object of securing as much income as possible from the pockets of the ships officers before we reached port. As the days wore on their plan seemed to work very well.

An LST (Landing Ship Tank) at sea.

We were soon taking our turn standing watch along with the ship's officers. There was no enemy action that we could be aware of from the deck of the LST. However, there were several days of rough, heavy seas. This led to the first of a number of sore points between the Army and Navy on that little ship. The majority of the ships complement was apparently just out of boot camp and many became violently ill from the heavy seas. The Army flyers were fresh from aerobatic training, and none got seasick.

Relations became more frosty as time went on. The card game had progressed as planned, and by the time we passed Gibraltar the Navy's attitude had become distinctly unfriendly. When we reached the convoys first port of call, which turned out to be Bizerte, North Africa, we were debating whether or not we should ask the Navy to put us ashore when we discovered that the crew was already throwing our baggage on the dock. We had arrived at our first stop on our way to the war.

Once we were ashore, our troop commander got in touch with the local military authority and was told they knew nothing about us. He managed to get in touch with the military at Tunis. They knew nothing about us either, but agreed to send some six by sixes, heavy trucks used by the Army for transport of troops and supplies, to pick us up. Some of us slept at the Red Cross club that night; I'm not sure where the rest went. The trucks arrived about midmorning, and we reached Tunis that afternoon. We were assigned austere quarters and went to an outdoor movie that night. I still remember, it was the old black and white film "Union Pacific" that I'd gone to see a few short months earlier with my family back in the tiny theater in Frankfort, Kansas.

Truck Convey in North Africa

We wandered around Tunis for three or four days while our troop commander tried to reach someone in authority who would know where we were supposed to go. Finally, as a group, we went to the base commander and said, in effect, "Where do we go?" He said, "Well, I've got some friends in the 15th Air Force in Italy, and they are very short of fighter pilots." He went on to indicate that if we were interested in going up there, he would send us up in a couple of "Gooney Birds" (C-47s). We said, "Great!" And next morning we loaded up and took off for Southern Italy.

We flew into a strip at San Severro, the home at that time of the 31st fighter wing. They, in turn, put all 40 of us into six by sixes and carried us over to wing headquarters. We unloaded and entered a large building. It was old and constructed of stone as I remember. There was a large room right inside, and as we went in the door, a senior officer was briefing a small group of eight or ten replacement pilots.

Our arrival was unexpected. I don't remember his exact words, but they were something to the effect of, "Where the hell did you come from?!" When we identified ourselves as replacement fighter pilots, we were quite welcome. They were indeed short of pilots; apparently replacements had not been arriving fast enough to keep up with losses.

Unknown pilot. Any landing you walk away from

The 15th at that time was flying two types of fighter aircraft, the P-38 and the P-51. Because of our large number, we were pretty much given our choice. Although some of us had gone to twin-engine advanced training, we had all ended up going through the replacement training unit in the P-47. Consequently a majority of us opted for the P-51. There was some latitude given those who had gone through trading together and wanted to go to the same fighter base.

A home at last – The 325th

After our initial briefing, we located our luggage, sorted it out, loaded it in six by sixes, and departed. By about 5:30 that evening our small group was putting up its tents at our new fighter base and preparing to settle into our new home away from home. I doubt we could have accomplished all that in one day if we had possessed proper orders.

Officers' Living Area – Lesina

I found that I had joined the 318th Fighter Squadron, one of three squadrons (the 317th, the 318th, and the 319th) of the 325th Fighter Group. Through a series of "accidents" that I believe were guided by the hand of Divine Providence, I had ended up with a great outfit.

The 325th been in Italy approximately six months. It had spent most of 1943 fighting in North Africa, where it had arrived on 19 January 1943, when Air Corps pilots who had never before made a carrier takeoff flew their P-40s off the deck of the aircraft carrier Ranger and landed at an airdrome near Casablanca. The group flew its first combat mission on 17 April 1943. At the time my future outfit was flying that first mission, I was undergoing physical training and cram courses in math and other subjects while the Air Corps rushed to expand the flight training pipeline.

The 325th had distinguished itself in the North African campaign. While moving from base to base in Africa it became known as the "Checkertail Clan". I believe it was the first group in the Army Air Corps that was permitted to adopt any sort of markings that would identify it. The Flying Tigers were first, but they were not originally an Air Corps organization and they were permitted to keep their distinctive markings after they were integrated into the U.S. Army. Gen. Spatz himself had approved the distinctive marking for the 325th, which, after some experimentation, consisted of 14 inch squares of black and yellow on the vertical and horizontal tail surfaces of their P-40s.

325th Commander, Francis Langford, and Bob Hope. P-40 in background, 1943.

The 325th flew its last P-40 mission on 22 September 1943. About that time I was in basic flight training. The unit was withdrawn from combat for conversion to P-47s. With the longer range P-47s came assignment to the 15th Air Force with responsibility to protect the Fifteenth's heavy bombers on strikes against targets in northern Italy and deeper into Europe. On 9 December it moved the first of its aircraft from North Africa to "Foggia Main" in Italy. That base was overtaxed and on the 30th the 325th was moved 7 miles away to "Foggia One." Because that base was crowded with heavy bombers, the 325th moved its P-47s in March 1944, to Lesina, a remote field approximately 45 miles north, where it was based when my small group of replacement pilots arrived. At the time the move was made to Lesina, I was at Dover Delaware in the replacement training unit, training in P-47s.

P-47s of the 325th 1943.

In May 1944, shortly before we arrived unannounced, the group's P-47s had been replaced with the P-51 "Mustang." It made the conversion, according to the *History the Checkertail Clan*, without the loss of a single hour of combat operations. Once equipped with the Mustang, a superb high-altitude, long-range fighter, the 325th could escort 15th Air Force bomber formations deep into Fortress Europe - to any target that might be assigned.

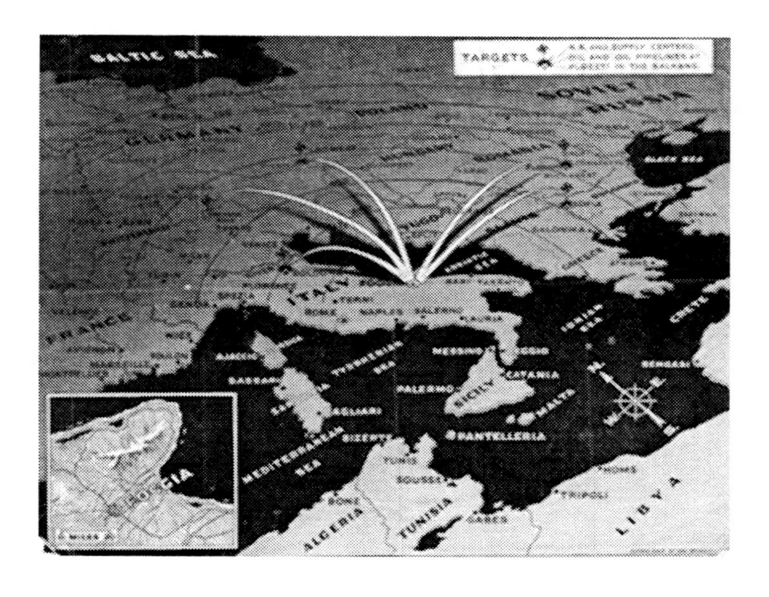

Some targets that might be assigned

The record of the 325th indicates that its target emphasis begin to shift in June 1944 to Axis oil supplies. For example, on the 16th it escorted B-24s to the Nova Oil Refinery at Schwechat, Austria. On the 23rd it flew to heavily defended Ploesti, Romania, where it took on 35 Nazi fighters and lost three P-51s while shooting down four enemy fighters. The next day it went back to Ploesti and shot down five, while losing one to Me-109s. Before the month ended, while flying a shuttle mission to Russia, it escorted eighth Air Force B-17s from Russia to Italy on their way back to

England. While escorting the bombers by way of Bucharest, the Checkertail Clan engaged 50 enemy fighters, downing 17 and losing none.

319th Operations Shack

In July, the month after I arrived, the 325th flew missions targeting the Reskos Locomotive Depot at Budapest, oil storage tanks at Giurgiu. Romania, refineries at Ploesti again, Verona's marshaling yards, the Bechhammer Oil Refinery in Germany, and various enemy airfields.

The memories of my first couple of missions are somewhat sketchy. As a green kid, I was fully occupied learning combat tactics and the operation of the P-51, which I had never flown before. This took all the attention a brand-new, 20 year old Mustang pilot could muster.

Puppies Vernon Bradeen and I adopted.

At the time our shipment of new pilots arrived, the 15th Air Force was losing experienced fighter pilots and raw replacements like us with some regularity, some to enemy fighters but more to the relentless German anti-aircraft guns, mechanical problems, and weather. Anti-aircraft defenses were heavy and the Germans' development of radar controlled guns made them highly accurate. On the return from one mission four of us were flying a fairly loose line abreast over an undercast. I was leading the flight and happened to be looking to my right just as two flack bursts blossomed between me and my element leader and two more bursts blossomed between him and his wingman. A few feet to either right or left and they would have gotten two aircraft without warning. We took sudden evasive maneuvers however and all of us escaped damage.

Losses of bomber crews were very high. As a fighter pilot, my combat tour was set at 50 missions. I believe the combat tour of the bomber crews was decreed by higher authority to be 35 missions, because only a shorter tour provided the bomber crews with any realistic hope of surviving the tour and going home.

Enemy fighters we could do something about, if we did our job of escort effectively. About the German anti-aircraft guns we could do little or nothing. My brother, the copilot on a 15th Air Force B-24 Liberator, once told me that when his plane flew over heavily defended targets, the bursts of smoke from antiaircraft shells exploding around his aircraft were so densely spaced that it almost seemed that a man could walk across the sky on them. And of course each burst was the source of deadly shrapnel that flew in all directions and easily penetrated aluminum aircraft skins and humans.

B-24 "Liberator" heavy bomber.

German fighters were dedicated to destroying the bombers. If it was necessary to destroy the bombers' fighter protection to do so, so be it. As replacement pilots fresh out of flight training, we encountered some highly skilled opponents.

My first P-51, a "C" model, had the older hinged canopy rather than the bubble canopy found on the later D models. The P-51 had an internal fuel tank installed right behind the armor plate behind the seat back. This tank held between 70 and 75 gallons. A full tank moved the center of gravity (CG) rearward to a point where the aircraft was unstable at certain attitudes. When we took off on a mission, we used fuel from this tank first, until it was down to about 35 gallons. Then the aircraft center of gravity was about where we wanted it to be. If the fuselage tank was burned empty, the CG moved forward, past the point where we wanted it for maximum maneuverability. We then switched the engine from the fuselage tank to one of the external wing tanks carried on bomb racks, one on each wing. They held 110 gallons each. On the outboard portion of the mission, we would switch back and forth between these tanks to keep the aircraft balanced.

P-51 With Drop Tanks

We would run these until they were nearly empty. Then it was necessary to begin to use the fuel stored in the internal wing tanks. The goal was to get as much range as possible out of the fuel in the external tanks, and to get it early, because they reduced speed, decreased maneuverability, and gave the enemy's bullets additional ignition sources to hit. We would bring the tanks back if we could, because they were reusable. A typical escort mission pattern went something like this: climb, cruise, meet bombers, escort as long as possible, leave the bombers, and arrive back at base with 15 to 20 minutes of fuel remaining. The escort leg might be for bombers inbound to the target, during their run over the target, or to cover their withdrawal. At times it might include all three. It all depended on the length of the bomber mission, where our planners thought the bombers would most likely encounter enemy fighters, and the availability of escort fighters. If enemy fighters bounced the bombers while they were in our charge, the tanks were dropped so we could engage the enemy.

I remember one occasion when we had to drop early. After the aerial battle was over I still had some ammunition left. On that particular day we had been instructed that if targets of opportunity were spotted - trucks, a train, etc. - we were to attack them. We were to disengage from that activity when our armament was exhausted or our fuel had been consumed to the point where it was time to head for home. I don't remember what the ground targets were that day, but I do recall that I was very busy (as they say today, "Time flies when you're having fun"). I do remember however that when I finished, the fuel gauge did not paint an excessively cheerful picture for the long trip home. I crossed the Adriatic where it was 75 to 80 miles wide, using best cruise control as we knew it, made a straight approach to our base which was very close to the shoreline, landed, and taxied directly to the revetment. The crew chief came in later and asked, "Did you know how much fuel your had?" "No, not really" I told him. I knew only that the needles had settled on empty and had stopped wiggling. He said that when he refueled the aircraft the tanks took within 3 ½ gallons of what the tech orders called for. In other words, they were empty.

A friend asked me years later what it felt like when I walked out to my Mustang for the first time. It felt great. My checkout ride in a single seat P-51 was much like my first ride in the P-47. An "experienced" P-51 pilot, who likely had only 30 to 40 hours in the machine himself, stood on the wing before I taxied out, and pointed out the various switches and knobs. I don't recall that we had any written operating instructions. They were in a hurry to get us checked out, because they really needed pilots in the air. Only days before my group of replacements arrived, shortly after the squadrons P-47s had been replaced by P-51s, the squadron had flown a mission to Avignon in southern France. It was a strafing mission against fierce defenses. Losses were heavy. The P-47s would have fared better on such a mission, but by then they were in workhorse use by the 12th Air Force.

With its low drag laminar flow wing, clean airframe, and Rolls-Royce Merlin engine, the P-51 possessed a remarkable combination of range and maneuverability, but it was quite vulnerable when used at low levels against well defended targets. After I returned from one mission, the crew chief and I took the cowling off because it had a bullet hole in it. We found that one metal cooling line had been creased by an enemy round and almost closed. If the bullet had impacted a fraction of an inch closer to the center of the line, it would almost certainly have ruptured and spilled coolant as fast as the pump could pump it out. The big Merlin engine was estimated to have a running time of only 60 to 90 seconds after coolant loss.

Mustang painted in the colors of Herky Green's P-51

With only one engine upfront, our pilots had to become very sensitive to the behavior of their power plants. On one mission I was flying the wing of our flight leader, Philip Sangermano, when he developed engine trouble over the Adriatic. He wanted an escort back to the coast of Italy. Inexplicably, as could happen, by the time we sighted the coast, the problem cleared up. Since it was too late to rejoin our group, we proceeded on back to base, beginning a cruising descent. There were two small islands just off the coast that we often flew over when departing from our base, but we had never seen them close up. As we approached them on the deck, the natural thing seemed to simply fly between them. We did so and continued at low level on to our base.

318th Squadron at Mission Briefing.

The next day, at the conclusion of our mission briefing, the group commander, Lieutenant Colonel Chet Sluder (whose Checkertail colors and aircraft number are today on a P-51 featured in the National Museum of the United States Air Force) stood up, as he sometimes did, to say a few additional words. That day, as closely as I can remember, in a very low-key way he said something like this, "Gentleman, the British contingent on the islands has requested that our P-51s not fly under the communication cables stretched between the islands." I turned to Phil, "Did you see any cables?" "No, did you?" The islands were far enough apart to allow two Mustangs to fly between them side-by-side with room to spare. I don't know how close to the water those cables sagged, but we didn't fly between the islands again.

Philip Sangermono was a dedicated and highly skilled fighter pilot. He was lost some days later and at about that time I was assigned as flight commander.

Most of our missions were bomber escort. On one such mission, I was flying wing for our squadron commander Sy Farnum. We were south of Vienna, escorting B-17s inbound to their target. Our Mustangs were flying above the bomber formation in broad S-curves to remain with the slower bombers. Me-109s were spotted far above us. They were not after us; they were after the B-17s. They dived vertically through us at the bombers. We could not prevent them from getting to the bombers, but we could go after them and keep them from making another pass. We rolled and dove after them through the bomber formation. Sy was on one Me-109's tail. We followed him, and he leveled out on the deck. I expect we chased him a few miles with Sy firing bursts at him. The Me-109 started to come apart, then rolled and went in.

Mustang painted in the colors of the P-51 Flown by Colonel Sluder. Located at the National Museum of the United States Air Force.

Checkertails escorting B-17s of the 99th Bomb Group

As the enemy 109s had dived through the box of B-17s, there was a B-17 that had its tail section separated from the rest of the fuselage. As we climbed back upstairs to rejoin the bomber force, passing through about 12,000 feet, we met the tail section of the B-17 lazily spiraling toward the ground. We did not know if it was the Me-109 that we shot down (I say "we" only because I was on Sy's wing) that had destroyed the bomber, but we hoped that it was.

The wingman stays with the lead so the guy whose wing he is flying on can devote his attention to offensive tactics. If the leader's guns jam, the wing man is in a position to carry on. That day I did not fire my guns. It was considered a serious technical offense to go "skylarking" - leaving the leaders wing.

Our escort missions often involved the B-24s of the 15th Air Force. My older brother's crew, who had named their B-24 the *Paper Doll* after a popular song of the day, was assigned to the 781st squadron, 465th group, 55th bomb wing. Robert ("Brother Buck" to me) had passed all the tests for the aviation cadet program before entering the Army, but the draft took him off our Kansas farm in early 1942, and he was sent to basic training and to the coast artillery. Orders to report to flying training caught up with him there, and he completed flight training approximately 6 months ahead of me in class 43-G.

We never knew until a mission briefing what heavy bombers we might be assigned to escort. We just did the best job we could, all the time, every time. In the heat of battle I saw many B-24s go down from enemy action, some aflame, some coming apart, some diving out of control. Some days we were assigned to escort 55th bomb wing B-24s. I never knew whether or not my brother's airplane might be among them.

On rare occasions such as a test hop, I was able to fly down to see my brother at his base. His tent was pitched partly up a low hill above the metal strips the B-24's operated from. I found that if I rolled my Mustang over to a nearly inverted position coming in over their strips, I can look through the open flaps of the tent and see if there was anyone about. On one occasion, although I saw no one, I had little extra time so I decided to land and see if he was on a mission. He was. On that day, seven B-24's from that squadron had gone on the mission. Two returned safely to base. Five did not. His is one of the five that did not return.

P-51s of the 325th Escorting B-24s

I waited as long as I could for word and took off an hour or so later and flew home, knowing only that he was likely dead or captured. It was not until later that I learned that two of the five missing aircraft had not gone down in enemy territory, but had made it back as far as an island, Vis, on the coast of Yugoslavia, which at that point was in the hands of Yugoslav partisans. His was one of the two. He later made it back to base (courtesy of the Partisans, with an assist from the U.S. Navy) where he and the rest of his crew soon manned another airplane and flew back into the battle.

These men took off for their missions in large, comparatively cumbersome aircraft, loaded to capacity with gasoline and bombs, and flew straight and level into heavily defended targets in the face of enemy fighters and anti-aircraft fire. The heroism they displayed, day after day, was a tribute to their courage, their sense of duty, and the way they were raised. I admire them to this day, just as I remain proud of my comrades, who flew their fighters in battle. Many fighter pilots were lost to enemy action of course, but their return to their base was not always without its problems. Sometimes an aircraft was alone. Weather could be a real problem. Navigation aids were primitive. There were no approach or landing systems. The crews in the bombers and the defenders in the fighters did it because they had a job to do. They knew that a world ruled by Nazis would be hell on earth for their loved ones, the end of our nation as we knew it, and the end of living under the principles on which our nation was founded.

I greatly admire the warriors in our volunteer armed forces today who put their lives on the line for their country. But their numbers are relatively small now, compared to the total population. In WW II a whole generation went to war. I wonder sometimes, if our country faced that kind of threat again, if it could find so many fine young men, with that kind of selfless courage, to stand between it and tyranny.

Personnel of the 318th, 1944.

I am grateful that my brother and his crew were among the survivors. It was a great day for me when I was able to fly up to his base and see him, now a hardened survivor of 35 missions, board a B-24, bound, not for another mission, but for home.

Of course the ones who actually flew the missions were only a part of the equation. The ground crews and other support people, who made the sustained effort possible under very difficult conditions, were fully as important.

Mechanics of the 318th working on a P-51

It was a distinct privilege to have been a member of the 325th Fighter Group. George Hamilton, another member the 325th, made the following comment to Herky Green some years later. They sum up my feelings about the unit as well, "It was a wonderful experience being with such a group of men. Nowhere since the war have I had the luck to be with the type of men we had, both officers and enlisted men. Everyone was a fully trained volunteer. All the enlisted men were highly skilled and a great many of them were very well educated. It just spoils you for the rest of your life to have to make do with a lesser level of skill and character with a resulting mediocrity."

Some years later I was fortunate enough to again be a member of an organization with similar attitudes and professionalism, the 85th Air Transport Squadron (heavy) in MATS in 1957-58, flying from Travis Air Force Base, but that's another story.

When the day finally arrived for the invasion of the South Coast of France, we were given a new role. Our group was assigned to escort "Gooney Birds" (C-47s) towing gliders full of troops and equipment. We staged at an airdrome on the west coast of Italy. We were briefed for the first mission in the predawn darkness and were off the ground about sunup. We met with the C-47s and stayed with them until, as I remember, they were almost to the drop area when the mission was recalled. We returned to Italy. After landing, while our ships were refueled, we ate and were briefed again, and took off to once again escort C-47s towing gliders up to southern France. They also staged from the West Coast of Italy. We caught up with them before they flew into enemy territory and escorted them in and out. This time they did drop their gliders. We encountered very minimum opposition. We returned to our staging base and landed just as the sun disappeared below the horizon. I found that I had spent 10 hours and 45 minutes in the cockpit of a P-51 that day. I still had my "C" model which was not as roomy as the "D" model with the bubble canopy that I flew later.

Major Hershel Green 1944.

P-51 Cockpit.

When the Germans were pulling out of Greece, up through Yugoslavia, we were ordered to attack their forces as they traveled north along the mountain roads. This required some rather interesting flying, following roads through winding river valleys, looking for targets of opportunity. On one occasion, strafing trucks or tanks on the road, (I don't recall which, perhaps because of what happened next) I concentrated too much on the task at hand and found myself heading upstream entering something like a box canyon without apparent room for escape. I pulled over a saddle just about stall speed, sort of hanging on the prop. It looked like I could have reached down and touched the trees. And of course the Germans were busy shooting at me. It was a bit disconcerting to look out and see bullet holes appearing in my wing.

Another mission that stands out in my memory occurred when our group was assigned to attack Ecka, an airdrome in Yugoslavia. It was fairly early in the morning, and we flew quite low into the target - low enough that we had a good splattering of bugs on our windscreens. The tactic worked. I don't believe any enemy aircraft got off the ground. There were 30 P-51s at the target area at 1000 hours. After an orderly start, in a few minutes it turned into a melee, with aircraft going in all directions. As I recall, I was able to make six passes over the field and was credited with three aircraft destroyed. I damaged additional aircraft, but that didn't really count. Reconnaissance photos later showed that every aircraft on the airdrome - fifty eight of various types - was destroyed, along with five more on a nearby airfield. We lost one P-51, apparently to ground fire.

Award of the Distinguished Flying Cross to Lt. John Gaston, 1944

After the Russians overran Hungary and liberated a large group of POWs, primarily Americans downed in raids on Ploisti, a number of B-17s were sent in to ferry people out. I led a flight of four Mustangs and escorted the last three B-17s to go in. While in the air overhead waiting for the B-17s to get loaded, we were bounced by a flight of Russian Yak-9s. They obviously knew that we were at maximum range. I'm as sure now as I was then that they did it to try to get us to drop our tanks. We didn't. They turned into us, and, as they did we turned into them. After about five passes they gave up and retired. They played a dangerous game. If there had been one wink of fire from one of their guns we would have opened up on them, with pleasure. But they didn't fire, and we didn't.

Lt. John Gaston Back from 50th Mission.

We stayed at low altitude over the field (2500 to 4000 feet) and the B-17s finally got off the ground about 30 minutes late. We followed them as long as we could. At that point we were so low on fuel that I elected to go into Lecce, a bomber base that was closer to our position than our home strip. When we landed, Les Long blew a tire when he was taxing in, probably hooking it on the edge of the steel matting. The aircraft was undamaged, but it was also not flyable. He did not wish to remain. Being quite small in stature, he left his chute, and by mutual consent with Hal Loftus, rode back to home base with Hal sitting on his lap flying the aircraft. I believe Vernon Bradeen was the fourth pilot of that flight.

My 50th mission, because it was my last, is very memorable to me. It was an escort mission to Regensburg in early February, 1945. The German Air Force by this time had been worn down and no enemy aircraft were encountered. The mission went off as programmed. All danger was not passed however. The Germans were very determined and their antiaircraft fire was still deadly.

My crew chief Pat Patterson told me, after I returned from Number Fifty, that I was his first pilot to complete fifty missions. He had been with the outfit since it landed in North Africa. Such are the fortunes of war, I guess, for Pat and my assistant crew chief, "Red" James, were the absolute finest in my opinion.

Lt. Gaston and his ground crew.

I returned to the states soon after. My combat tour with the Checkertail Clan was over. The 325th ultimately ended the war with a total of 578 missions, 525 aerial victories, 281 enemy aircraft destroyed on the ground, and 148 combat losses. Additional damage to the Nazi war machine included 47 aerial "probables", 93 damaged, and a large number of ground targets, including 264 locomotives, 159 motor vehicles, and 148 rail cars, primarily tank cars. The group had 27 aces, including Herky Green, who, when grounded by higher headquarters, was the leading ace in the 15th Air Force with 18 aerial victories. According to the history of the Checkertail Clan, the 325th flew its last combat mission about three months later, on 7 May 1945, a few hours before the end of the war in Europe. On that last mission, five Mustangs escorted Halifax bombers on a supply drop in open country. "On this quiet note" the Checkertail history reads, "The war came to an end for the 325th fighter group."

Chapter Three: Demobilization

After my final P-51 combat mission in the European theater, I was rotated back to the states from my base in Italy. Unlike my journey to Europe, which had been aboard an LST (landing ship tank) as part of a large slow convoy, I and a few others flew home not in a grand transatlantic flight as might take place today but in a series of shorter hops. First, from Southern Italy by C-46 to a desert strip at Atar in North Africa to refuel, and then on to Dakar, Senegal. Then in a shiny new C-54, with canvas seats along both sides of the fuselage, to Natal, Brazil, where we boarded a C-87. The C-87 was basically a B-24 similar to that flown by my older brother Robert during his combat tour. This B-24 did not carry machine guns and bombs. The combat gear had been deleted and passenger seats installed. We rode in comparative luxury then to Georgetown, British Guiana, to Puerto Rico, and on to Miami, Florida. The USA at last!

I bought a train ticket to Malone, New York to pick up the wife I had met and married days before going overseas, and then it was back down the coast to a processing center at Atlantic City, again by train. As I recall, I had to buy my own ticket and the government reimbursed me something like three cents a mile for travel. The army warehoused returning flyers there while they waited, usually only a few days, for orders. When the orders came through they were for Craig Field at Selma, Alabama, where I was to be placed in instructor school. I expected, following that, to be instructing basic training in the AT-6. While I was at Selma, the war in Europe ended and the Army Air Corps turned its full attention to the coming campaign in the Pacific. The Army Air Corps intended to get maximum mileage out of its combat veterans by using them, first as instructors, and then as seasoning in new combat units being prepared for the war in the Pacific. While I was at Selma a request came in for P-47 instructors in Texas. I volunteered and was ordered to Majors Field at Greenville, Texas.

Flying was in my blood, and the P-47N was a pilot's dream, but I was not necessarily looking forward to another combat tour. After missions to Ploesti and other hot spots in Europe, the idea of escorting B-29s on missions from air bases located on tiny islands, over hundreds of miles of deep pacific in a single engine aircraft to the Japanese Homeland and back was not particularly appealing.

At Greenville, a levy came in for an instructor pilot to attend a gunnery school at Galveston, Texas. I was ordered there, and after a week (I had not begun training) my wife hated the South Texas bugs and the one room we had for temporary quarters. I requested a return to Greenville. The problem continued after I returned to Greenville. She made it plain that she had grown tired of several things: living out of a suitcase, the minimal housing that was available in the communities adjacent to busy training bases, and a service life that somehow did not match her dreams. She also made it plain that her plans had not included my returning alive from the war. I was granted emergency leave to drive her to Topeka, Kansas for her to catch a train to New York.

I remained until I could get her on a train, and then drove back to Greenville. When I arrived that Monday morning, the field was almost deserted. Within a span of ten days, instructors, pilots, ground crews, and aircraft were gone. Most had been ordered to Abilene, Texas, another P-47 training base. I was ordered to remain for a short time, about thirty days I think, whereupon I was to follow the training activities to Abilene.

We were never allowed to stay put very long. In fact, soon after arrival in Abilene, I was ordered to Avenger Field in Sweetwater, Texas to continue training pilots in the P-47N. The aircraft I had flown in Europe, North American's superb P-51 Mustang, due to its combination of high performance and range, was the dominant U.S. fighter. The P-47D models in service in late 1943 lacked the range to penetrate very far beyond the western border of Germany and they were assigned to be tactical fighter-bombers, a role that rugged aircraft performed very well.

In the vast Pacific, a fighter would need a true combat radius of at least 1,000 miles, but the P-47D did not have the range to go that distance, fight, and return to base. However, at Republic Aviation, designers and mechanics had been busy fitting 27 inch long extension inserts in each wing of a test aircraft to evaluate the handling. They found that the modifications hurt the roll rate, so the wings were clipped and squared off at the tip. Initially, no provision was made to carry additional fuel in the wings. But in May of 1944, Republic was given approximately $100,000 to develop a "wet" wing. The inserts were shrunk to 18 inches and an integral fuel tank for 100 gallons of fuel put in each insert. The P-47N was born.

The new prototype was flown in mock combat with the P-47 D, and bested its older brother in every category of performance. A more powerful engine made it the world's fastest production, propeller driven fighter, with long range. In a test flight from Farmingdale to Elgin Field in Florida, the XP-47N had taken off at a whopping gross weight of 20,166 lbs, with 600 gallons of usable fuel in two drop tanks hanging from under-wing hard points. It flew to Florida accompanied by a P-47D chase plane, dropped its tanks, engaged in a 20 minute mock dogfight with a P-47D waiting at Eglin, turned around, and headed for home. After a weather diversion, it ended its 1,980 mile marathon at Woodbine, New Jersey, having used 1,057.5 gallons of fuel, with enough fuel in its main tank for another 300 plus miles. The P-47N was ready for the Pacific.

In the turmoil of World War Two pilots might think they knew what they would be flying when they got to the combat theater. But, although I had been trained to fly the P-47 before being shipped overseas, I had ended up in Italy where I flew the P-51Mustang in combat. Now I was going to be a P-47 instructor. If it had not been for difficult personal circumstances, for a kid who always wanted to fly, to continue flying in the most advanced fighter of its time, would have been a little like heaven on earth.

I should add here a brief note about a challenging part of my training to be an instructor in the P-47. My fellow combat veterans and I, who had not flown the Thunderbolt in combat, had to demonstrate instrument proficiency in the P-47 before we were considered fully qualified instructors. There were no navigational aids to speak of at that time, and no dual-control P-47s, so the Air Corps had figured out a unique way to test our skills. The person being checked out took off with an experienced instructor on his wing. Following gear retraction, the check ride instructor, who was flying right on my wing said something like, "All right, pull your goggles down." Since he was right on my wing he could see exactly what his student was doing. I forget exactly how the colors red and green were arranged, but the goggles were either red or green, and the canopy had some colored plastic of the other color taped inside it. When the goggles were pulled down the outside world disappeared and I was alone in the cockpit with only controls and instruments visible. The instructor stayed on my wing while I performed a complex set of maneuvers at his command - climbs, descents, turns, stalls and stall recoveries, and probably others I do not recall now. When he was satisfied he gave me a heading and we flew back to base. He gave me headings, turns, and rates of descent, and at the critical moment radioed, "OK, push your goggles up." We were some 200 feet over the runway, just as if we had broken out of the clouds on a perfect instrument approach. I made a routine landing.

Somewhere in this period of confusion I had to make a cross country flight in the P-47, it seems like it was Topeka. In any event I passed fairly close to my old home town. Now, as it happened, back when we were in high school some of us had talked about possibly getting to fly some day, and if we did, we agreed then that we would have a solemn obligation to buzz Frankfort. Well there I was in that beautiful Thunderbolt with its Pratt & Whitney R-2800 Double Wasp, two-row, 18-cylinder radial roaring up front. What would you have done? The town was about a mile square in extent. The north-south main street started in the low ground at the south edge of town and climbed a hill to where the high school stood. When I made that run from south to north I suddenly realized how small that town really was. I doubt anyone in town that day will ever forget that buzz job.

While in Greenville, I had traded my 1938 De Soto for a 1941 Chevy Club Coupe.

I drove it to Avenger Field where I expected to plunge again into the role of instructor pilot. But when I got there they said, "We have plenty of instructors, but with your experience you will be invaluable as the Assistant Base Operations Officer."

I was at Avenger Field when V-J Day came at 6:10 p.m. EDT on 14 August 1945. Although the formal surrender ceremony in Tokyo did not occur until 2 September, we knew the war was over. The Potsdam Conference had offered a simple choice - surrender unconditionally or risk total annihilation. Japan refused, but after the U.S dropped atomic bombs on Hiroshima and Nagasaki the Emperor overruled fanatic military leaders and ended the war.

V-J day came as a great relief, not only to Air Corps personnel like us, but to thousands of soldiers and marines, as well as naval personnel, who were being assembled at island bases in the Pacific and ports in the United States, to take part in what would be a bloody push against Japan itself.

Japanese military brass expected one thousand Japanese and American soldiers to die every hour. How many civilians would have committed suicide in their homes or in mass military attacks is a number we can only guess at. Intelligence studies and military estimates made 50 years ago clearly indicate that the battle for Japan would likely have been the biggest bloodbath in the history of modern warfare.

As it was, the one million, and probably many more, young Americans otherwise destined to die in the battle for Japan lived. The war ships and transports scheduled to carry the invasion troops to Japan instead carried them home.

Whatever present day critics may say about atomic weapons and the way they were employed, it is a fact that, as awful as they were, for every death they caused, they led to many more Japanese lives being saved as a result of the quick ending of the war. And many young Americans returned home safely, men who would have died in the oceans off Japan and on its beaches.

At Avenger Field, following V - J Day, the situation was chaotic. Airplanes were flown out, and personnel ordered elsewhere. As Assistant Operations Officer I was one of two commissioned officers left on base. I suppose, technically, because I was rated, I was the base commander and I suddenly had to sign for a bunch of stuff. I was alone with an AT-6, a radio operator, a mechanic, one other enlisted man, and a Major, the transportation officer. Maybe he was angry because he felt he should have been in charge. Or maybe he was just in a hurry to leave. Whatever the reason he ordered a huge amount of the stuff I was signed for loaded on trucks and shipped out. If it had not been for that one remaining aircraft I don't know what I would have done. I flew that little airplane to bases all over Texas and Oklahoma until I had tracked down all the material I had been charged with. Then, in October 1945, I closed the base.

It was a joyous time, but it had a sad sight for anyone who loved airplanes. At Tinker Field in Oklahoma I saw row upon row of shiny new P-47s, as close as they could be shoved, one against the other, tipped up on their noses, tail feathers in the air, waiting to be destroyed. Fortunately I was not around to see bulldozers crush those beautiful birds to scrap.

I received orders to Clovis, New Mexico, but before I could wind down the property mess at Avenger Field, I was ordered instead to La Junta, Colorado. From there I was sent to Michigan, to Selfridge Field just north of Detroit. The war was over, but there was a lot of housekeeping to be done - very serious housekeeping that dealt with American families coping with grief over loved ones lost in the war and often tangled financial affairs to unravel. I was assigned as a personal affairs officer, with a car, driver, and two stuffed file cabinets. Each folder in the cabinets represented a soldier who had lost his life or was still listed as missing in action. I was responsible for helping families in Michigan, Northwestern Ohio, and Northeastern Indiana get the affairs of these young men in order. It was sober work, but significant.

Selfridge Field was a fighter base, and two elite P-47 fighter units were being formed there, the 56th and the 4th. I don't recall now if they were designated as groups or squadrons. Both were headed up by seasoned commanders with distinguished combat records: the 56th by Dave Shilling, and the 4th by E. H. Beverly who had been one of the commanders of the 325th fighter group, my combat unit in Europe. The selection process was just that, very selective. It included review of the combat records of would-be members and personal interviews. I was selected for the 4th. It was a distinct honor, and I looked forward eagerly to the arrival of our P-47Ns and training as a part of this elite combat unit.

A notable individual at Selfridge was Colonel Hank Spicer. As I heard the story, Colonel Spicer and been the senior officer at a POW camp in Germany. The Germans became agitated over a speech he gave to his fellow prisoners and condemned him to death. Readers may have heard stories of POW camps being bombed and the prisoners escaping. This, so the story goes, was one of those times. Along with other prisoners, Colonel Spicer escaped and avoided execution. One morning when I was at work, and this is still vivid in my memory, Colonel Spicer came by and said "John, get a chute. We're going to fly. There's a little community down the road that wants an air show, and we're going to give it to them." We did. It was a lot of fun. He was quite a guy.

I had worked through all the files in the cabinets and our planes still had not arrived. The personnel officer called me. He had an opening for the Army Information School at Carlisle Barracks in Pennsylvania and asked if I was interested. I was interested in learning all I could, so I volunteered. It was the best school I ever attended. It was intense. My fellow students were newspaper editors, screen writers, publicists, and other journeymen who had gone directly from responsible positions in civilian life into World War Two's citizen army. In three months there I learned a lot that I used throughout my career and much that I remember to this day.

When I returned to Selfledge Field on a Monday morning I was greeted with the statement, "We don't know whether to say hello or goodby." A TWX had come in Sunday afternoon with a long list of names of people to be discharged. My name was on the list. Orders had arrived hours later, early Monday morning, assigning me to Weather School in commissioned status.

I very much wanted to stay in the Army Air Corps somehow, and continue to fly. It seemed to me to be what I was born to do, and I knew I had a lot to contribute. But it was not to be. I called the Air Weather Service to see if they could negate the RIF notice. They asked one question, "Do you have a degree? Any kind of degree?" It could have been in anything from Ancient Languages to Basket Weaving and it would not have mattered. It would have been a degree. But I had gone directly from high school to flight training to combat. There was no opportunity for anything else. Their answer, "There's nothing we can do for you."

The base personnel officer called me. He said, "John, you are a fine young officer. You belong in the service. I would do anything I could for you, but I have received my separation orders too."

Facing imminent discharge, I took my new wife and headed for Sweetwater, Texas, her home, but on the way stopped by the Headquarters of the Continental Weather Wing at Tinker Field near Oklahoma City. I will never forget the businesslike but thoughtful reception I received from the Deputy Commander, Colonel Paul Norton. He went over my service record and said "You are the kind of people we want in the Air Weather Service." He noted that when I was commissioned, people like me at that time were given a "Master Sergeant letter", that gave us the right to enlist at the rank of Master Sergeant if RIFed from commissioned status. Colonel Norton instructed me that if I elected to do that, I should drive up and enlist there at Headquarters, Continental Weather Wing. They would send me to meteorology school.

I drove to Texas and surveyed the civilian job market, looking for the best way to support my family. I elected to do just as Colonel Norton had instructed. I drove to Tinker and enlisted. I was assigned temporarily to on-the-job training in the base weather station, and at the first opportunity sent to Weather Observer Training at Chanute Field in Illinois. Then it was back to Tinker, and then back to Chanute, where I completed training and graduated as a Weather Forecaster on 17 December 1947.

Flying training was finished. A combat tour in Europe with the finest fighter pilots on the face of the earth was finished. My selection to be a member of an elite fighter unit was for nothing. And a pell mell demobilization was finished. I began a new segment of my career as an enlisted weather forecaster. I was embarking on a new career that would bring me face to face with the good and bad of service in the enlisted ranks, intense training in the fields of meteorology and communications, and valuable experience as a weather forecaster.

I assumed my duties as a Master Sergeant and fully qualified weather forecaster. The day I walked into the station at Tinker after completing school, the Station Commander, Major E. J. Fawbush, who I had learned was a forecaster of the first rank, threw me a set of keys and said, "John, the weather station is yours. You are now station chief. I will be here if you need me, but Miller and I have something to work on." Captain Miller was a mathematician, a very good one. The two of them put the lessons they had learned over distinguished careers into a form that would survive rigorous scrutiny. Together they created for the Air Force its first Severe Weather Forecasting System, the first big insight into tornado weather forecasting. That spring, they correctly forecast two periods of such activity, both of which saw destructive tornados in the immediate area of the Base, one of which I had personal experience with.

My wife, three year old adopted son, and I were living in a mobile home (we called them trailer houses in that day, and that is what they were - small and not at all substantial. I was off duty in the evening looking out the window into the darkness when a flash of lightning lit up an approaching funnel cloud. There was a Douglas Aircraft Company refurbishing plant near the base, and the swirling winds had picked up a four engine C-54 like it was a toy, and thrown it into the air just as the lightning flashed. I will never forget the sight of that large aircraft; I saw the silhouette as it lifted on its side and started into the air just as if I had been looking down on it from above - fuselage, wing and all four engines plainly outlined.

We dashed out of the trailer house to the nearest ditch. I pushed my son into the small space under a foot bridge, threw my wife into the ditch, and covered her with my body. The wind tore at us and the rain and hail pelted us, but the funnel went on by. My son started screaming because the cold water was rising and soaking him. I grabbed him up and ran to the bathhouse and held him under a warm shower until he stopped shaking from the cold.

Our little home escaped the damage. Some of the trailer houses in the little trailer park were badly damaged. Not too many months after that we received a dream assignment - to Bermuda. Although it was cut short by family circumstances, it turned out to be an intense and interesting job in a busy weather station.

The weather station was being manned by three highly competent civilians working for a government contractor. The three military replacements had only about a week overlap to learn the procedures before their employer shipped them to new assignments. Housing was scarce but one of them was renting a small house (it seemed like everything was small in Bermuda - small but usually beautiful) from a local couple. We arranged to rent the house, and stayed with the fine British couple, who became lifelong friends, until the house was vacated. The civilian forecaster who was leaving the house also had a bicycle with a small gasoline engine mounted on the frame, driving the rear wheel with a belt. It was called a "Whizzer", and I rode it to work for several months, until unfortunate circumstances forced a transfer.

The work was intense and responsible. The weather station was manned 24 hours a day and the three of us each had responsibility for one eight hour shift. We were responsible for all weather briefings and weather forecasts for U.S. military flights, foreign military flights, and the American and Foreign commercial flights departing the island. I recall Pan Am, British South African Airlines, Colonial, TWA, Canada's National Air Line, and Mexico's. And there were many others. There were many military flights to Europe, including a regular rotation of B-29s to England from bases in the U.S. and back.

Frankly, we worked like dogs. Each 24 hour period we were required to prepare four surface maps, a 500 milibar chart, an 850, and two 700 milibar charts. We provided weather briefings to all departing flights, and predicted weather conditions for the entire flight. When we consider that, unlike today, almost all flights were low and slow (160 to 200 miles per hour) a typical flight to the Azores, a speck in the ocean where many flights went next from Bermuda, routinely took ten to eleven hours, that gave the weather ample opportunity at the destination to change during the flight. We were required to send to that next destination our prediction of the likely weather for the last half of the flight so the receiving station could notify the aircraft in transit if there had been any significant changes during the flight.

I looked forward to a three year tour in Bermuda but it was not to be. We had been on station less than a year when my wife's father became seriously ill and passed away. I expected that she would visit the family and return, however, once there, she informed me she had decided to remain there for the balance of my tour. I was faced with the prospect of being separated from wife and son for two years. So I decided the thing to do was volunteer for a remote location which would involve a short tour of only one year, and then a return to the States.

Some weeks before I was to depart, however, I received a letter directly from Headquarters U.S. Air Force. There was an urgent need for experienced pilots, and if I wished to be recalled to commissioned flight status I was to reply directly to Headquarters by letter expressing a willingness to be recalled voluntarily. This was my opportunity to fly again.

I received the letter at my duty station, and since it was from Headquarters, I opened it immediately. And then began one of the most frustrating experiences in my entire service as an enlisted troop. Just as I was reading it the detachment commander walked by. Asking what it was, he directed me to hand it to him so he could read it. He took it, read it, and said, "John, I want to put an endorsement on your reply." I told him it was not necessary since I was directed to send my reply directly to Headquarters. He insisted. I was a sergeant, he was a Lieutenant Colonel. I prepared my reply indicating my willingness to be recalled, and somewhat reluctantly gave it to him to forward hoping it would not be delayed since Headquarters required an immediate response. In the next few days, with orders to report to Greenland, I asked him a number of times if he had sent the letter on. He always said no, but he would get to it. The day before I was to leave I asked him again. As I recall he said something like, "No, Damn it, but I will do it tomorrow." I flew out for Westover Field in Massachusetts on the 10th of December 1948.

After I had been on duty for some time at BW1 in Greenland, the commander of our weather Group conducted a visit of our weather station. In conversation, he asked me why I did not apply for recall to active duty. I told him I had, but had not received a reply to my letter. He told me that he was headed for Washington, and would find out. He looked into the matter and told me by letter that he had discovered the Bermuda Detachment Commander had held the letter for approximately three additional weeks (until 31 December) before sending it forward - and instead of sending it directly to headquarters as directed, he had sent it on a tortuous route through channels, which took additional days.

Had he permitted me to apply directly as I had been directed, I would have been recalled to flying status as a commissioned officer and flying in the Berlin Airlift. Why would anyone deliberately scuttle my opportunity for recall? Whatever the reason, it set my career back. Did it affect his? All I know is that he received no further promotions before retirement. Years later, after I was recalled to flying status and serving as an aircraft commander in flights across the Pacific, he showed up on the passenger manifest one dark, stormy night. When I greeted him in the terminal and he learned I was the aircraft commander, he seemed to turn pale, and was unable to speak clearly. I did not see him again. All I know is that he cancelled the opportunity to take the flight.

I finished my one year tour in Greenland without incident. Concerned about the welfare of my family at home, I sent home what money I could so my wife could add it to the allotment she received directly. I found two opportunities to earn extra money - cutting hair and setting pins at the bowling alley, and dutifully sent home whatever I could make that way.

While I was there, one friend rotated back to the states, going through Nebraska he stopped in to tell my mother I was doing well and described me as the "sparkplug of our basketball team". I found out later that visit meant a lot to her.

Chapter Four: Commissioned Service

In his novel *Glory Road,* Robert A. Heinlein, the Dean of Science Fiction, had this to say, "Regardless of T.O., all military bureaucracies consist of a Surprise Party Department, a Practical Joke Department, and a Fairy Godmother Department." (The first two departments are always larger than the third, which is quite small.) I suspect that most servicemen and women have experienced each of the three at some time during their career, particularly with regard to their duty assignments.

After years of frustration in attempts to apply for recall in commissioned status, one bright day I received an envelope with no explanation and no cover letter, just a sheaf of orders. I was recalled to active duty as an officer in non-rated status. Was this a result of a previous application, or simply the output of what must have been the Fairy Godmother Department at Headquarters, Air Force Reserve? There was no way to tell. This was in March, 1951. I was directed to report to Patrick Air Force Base in Florida on 1 April.

The Air Force had taken over the old Navy Banana River Base and the base was bristling with activity in support of the Missile Test Range at Cape Canaveral. When I arrived, the job I was slated for had been filled and personnel suggested that the base needed a club officer. When they understood my reluctance to go there they said there was a possibility Base Supply could use me. When I inquired there, the answer was an enthusiastic, "Yes, we need you!" It was an interesting job. Supplies arrived daily destined for the Missile Test Center. A number of fine people worked in my three branches: Receiving and Shipping, Inspection, and Packing and Crating. I cannot specify how many people reported to me because the number was always changing, people were always coming in and going out, but the number was considerable. After verification I had to personally sign the receiving reports for all shipments that came in; it was a very responsible position.

About this time I received an interoffice memo from Base Personnel telling me that all my previous Military Occupational Specialty Codes (each was called an MOS) would be deleted and I would be assigned the MOS for a fully qualified Supply Officer. Not only was I not a fully qualified Supply Officer, although I was learning the job as rapidly as possible, that would delete from my record official recognition that I was a rated officer. Apparently this was unofficial policy because it prevented urgent levies for personnel qualified in other areas from being honored. Officially, personnel assigned there would no longer be qualified to fill such levies. The practice was doubtless effective, but illegal. When told at personnel there was no recourse I turned, walked out, and went immediately to the office of the Air Inspector. I said, "They can't do that". He said, "They can't do that". Four days later all my hard-earned MOSs were restored.

Unfortunately, this effort to retain my hard-earned Military Specialty Codes had made waves, big ones, and I knew my name was mud in that organization. Back to personnel where I asked, in plain terms, "How do I get out of here?" The only way was to apply for a school that required a permanent change of station (PCS). There was only one school available: Communications and Electronics at Scott Field in Illinois. I said, "Put me down" and they did. It was a year-long school.

Just before leaving Patrick, I discovered it was possible to apply to return to flying status. I took and passed the required physical exam and submitted the paperwork.

While at Scott, I inquired about being awarded the Officer Weather MOS. I was told that I must meet a classification board, which I did, and was awarded that MOS.

In September 1952, after completing the year-long Communications Officer Training Course, I was assigned to Davis Monthan Air Force Base at Tucson, Arizona, as a communications officer. Upon arriving at Davis Monthan, I was told I would be on station for one and a half years. That seemed fine to me. Four days later a TWX arrived ordering me to duty as a Weather Officer with the North East Air Command. I hooked up my trailer, which I had towed to Arizona, and pulled it to Lubbock, Texas, where I parked it at my brother's house. I traveled to my assignment at Pepperell Air Force Base at St. John's, Newfoundland, where it was proposed that I be assigned as Detachment Commander at BW3, a little weather station at the mouth of the Fiord that led up to BW1 where I had been stationed before. I guess you could say they wanted me back home in Greenland.

"Wait" I said, "I just got back from a remote tour and should not be assigned to a remote spot again". "No, I guess you're right." So I was assigned to a vacant position as Communications Officer at Pepperell AFB, Newfoundland. Shortly after arrival at Pepperell, additional orders came restoring me to flight status. Was this a response to my application or a result of some new policy? I do not know, but the restoration was more than welcome! There was a flying section assigned to the communications organization. It had a C-54 and a C-47. Their function was to help train GCA (Ground Control Approach) operators and check the operation of navigational aids throughout the Northeast Air Command. For flying I was directly attached to this aviation section.

The C-47 "Skytrain" (Gooney Bird)

What an excellent opportunity to fly and improve my weather proficiency! The equipment was good and professionally maintained. And I flew with superb pilots. The commander of the air unit was Thadius Phillips. He was an excellent officer. We called him "Big Phil" and he was the boss. I still recall names of the three excellent pilots I flew with: Lee B. Eddington, Mark Fjelsted, and Kenneth Gunnerson. I did not qualify as aircraft commander during that period and always flew as co-pilot, but it was an opportunity to gain experience in flying aircraft considerably larger than the P-47s and P-51s I had flown during WW II and to learn from fine pilots, flying in weather that was more often bad than good!

It seems as if the military services have a tradition of responding to budgetary pressures by cutting personnel, only to expand during the next critical time - something in the manner of a yo-yo going up and down. The impact on the career personnel involved appears to be considered of little consequence. The time was 1953, and a new Reduction in Force (RIF) list came out. I was not on it. Someone informed me however - I don't recall who - that the name of my immediate boss in the communications office was. The next duty day, a Monday, I went into his office to express my regret at the news. His reaction was a total surprise: "It's a damn good thing the list didn't come out after your last OER or you would be on the list instead of me!" I was dumbfounded. Two weeks before, after carefully evaluating my performance, he had gone over my effectiveness report with me. It was excellent. Now, he continued, "Oh, here's the one that went in!" I looked at it. It was terrible. It turned out that he had rewritten the report on Friday or Saturday and had it hand carried by a man who was going to AACS on Sunday.

He had apparently forgotten that he had given me a draft of the first report and the notes he had used to write it up. The report he showed me in his office that Monday morning was a career-killer; I could not let it stand. I went immediately to the Personnel Officer and said, "I want an appointment with the commander and I want you to be there." He set up the appointment.

The commander's response, as I recall, was on the order of, "This is terrible. I'll tell you what. I am going to Washington next week. I will find that OER and will correct all this."

As the country song says, "After that it just wasn't real pretty." It became increasingly clear that I had a target painted on my back. The supervisor of the man who had rewritten my OER was a lieutenant colonel. One morning we were having a torrential downpour. (St. John's, Newfoundland had its share of rain.) I normally arrived early but that morning I had a flat tire. After jacking the car up and changing the tire in the downpour - because I normally got to work very early - even with the delay I arrived only seven minutes late. Within two minutes I was in his office - in a brace - being chewed out for being late. It was obvious that he fully supported the man who had rewritten my OER.

Recognizing that the situation was desperate I did the only thing possible, went to the Personnel Office and made it plain that I could not and would not work for the man who had rewritten the negatively-slanted effectiveness report. Fortunately, there was a vacancy, the position of Assistant Navigation Aids Plans Officer and I qualified because of my additional duty with the Aviation Section.

It was clear however that for the health of my career, I needed to be completely gone from that organization. My directed duty assignment of one year was about up. The commander at Fifth Weather Group Headquarters, upon inquiry said, in effect, "We would be glad to have you. Put in an application for transfer." The organization was fairly new and staffing was in progress. Interestingly, the Colonel in charge of the AACS Group (or perhaps it had become a Wing by this time, I am not sure) also was the Senior MATS officer in the Northeast Air Command and had the authority to approve the transfer. I am sure to this day that he simply felt, "We need to get rid of this guy." Why? He was between a rock and a hard place. I learned later that before I walked into his office with evidence of the altered OER, he had been aware of the fact that my boss was on the RIF list and had gone to bat for him. He had not signed the bogus OER but his deputy had, so he had responsibility. Further, on his trip to Washington, he had not taken action to correct that OER. In fact, years later, in 1958, I had the opportunity to read the endorsement he had added to my OER. It was even more derogatory than what my immediate supervisor had said when he submitted the suddenly-revised OER.

I reported to the Weather Squadron and was assigned as a Meteorologist. At this point they were forming a Forecast Central and after about a month I was the only rated forecaster in the unit. They had set up a base out at Torbay Airport to serve the Northeast Air Command. Its parent unit was Northeast Air Command Headquarters located at Pepperell AFB at St. John's Newfoundland. I was assigned to the airport at Torbay and remained there for approximately two years, for the duration of my tour. Torbay was an international clearing station. We handled a lot of foreign aircraft - both civilian and military. At the weather station, we had enlisted observers and forecasters who were both enlisted men and officers, in sufficient numbers to run a 24 hour operation with three shifts. We had a Raywinsonde station that used balloons to check such things as upper wind direction and velocity, humidity, dew point, and so forth. This was vital information because we had the responsibility to predict weather over the open sea where there were very few observation stations. We also had a relatively new system. The acronym was SFERICS and I do not recall the exact name. It had large antennas and its function was to track and record lightning strikes, a distinct help in keeping track of the location of thunderstorms over the ocean. It was a responsible job and I had a group of very competent men. I was very fortunate that a highly competent individual, Master Sergeant Martin Grant, was in charge of the SFERICS system.

This assignment required that I function directly and closely with the Base Operations Officer, the Air Base Wing, and other aviation people at Torbay, and also as Staff Weather Officer to the 6622nd Air Transport Squadron. A benefit was that I was welcome to fly with the latter whenever I could get loose. I also continued to fly with the AACS Flight Check Squadron. At this time I was checked out as Aircraft Commander in the C-47.

I enjoyed the challenges of this assignment but the time for expected transfer was drawing near. Consequently, I put in a request, still within the Air Weather Service, to fly WB-50s, as they were called, flying regular tracks over the Atlantic and doing hurricane penetrations. It was not to be. Once again, I was ordered to Davis Monthan Air Force Base at Tucson, Arizona as a Weather Officer. There I was a staff officer for the 47th Bomb Wing which flew B-47s and KC-97 tankers. As I recall the Air Defense

Command (ADC) had a squadron of F-86 interceptors there (probably the D version but I do not recall). The Air Base Wing flew both the C-47 and the C-45 Twin Beech, and, attached for flying there, I checked out as aircraft commander in both.

After some time had passed, a TWX arrived from Headquarters Air Force saying, in effect, "We are going to clip your wings." My reaction? "Don't do that!" But how could it be prevented? I checked the regs and discovered that an officer who wished to remain on flying status could apply to Headquarters Air Force for flying duty. This was implementation of a policy to provide low time pilots an opportunity to build up their time and cockpit experience. The application had to go through channels of course but each layer of command had to send it on until it arrived at Air Force Headquarters. An intermediate command could not derail it. I submitted an application without delay! My immediate organization recommended disapproval and Air Weather Service recommended disapproval, but MATS said there were no grounds to disapprove it. It looked like I could be headed for the WB-50s I had applied for earlier, or for C-124 transports. The Air Weather Service said, in effect, "OK, this guy can go to C-124s but in two years we want him back" and cut orders directing me to C-124 school at West Palm Beach, Florida with subsequent assignment to Travis Air Force Base near Fairfield, California.

This meant that I would be leaving the Air Weather Service. The weather people at Davis Monthan were assigned to a headquarters at March Air Force Base in California. At this point two senior officers from March flew up to Davis Monthan, walked into base operations (not even into the weather station) called me out and proceeded to dress me down, in public, in front of the personnel on duty and those passing through. They asked me loudly if I was a coward because I did not want to remain in the Air Weather Service and fly WB-50s. My reaction? Suppressed anger of course, but more than that the feeling that it was a sad thing indeed that two senior commissioned officers would apparently take it upon themselves to chastise a lowly captain - in public - just because he had the nerve to leave the Air Weather Service. They had not bothered to inform themselves that I had applied for WB-50 duty and been turned down twice, and, whether they had or not, my transfer did not call for such action on their part.

The C-124 "Globemaster" (Old Shaky)

Is for me, it was on to Patrick Air Force Base and instruction in flying that mammoth bird, the C-124.

Words cannot fully describe the pleasure it gave me to be back in the flying business. The C-124 was huge compared to anything I had ever flown before, but it was still an airplane, and I quickly grew comfortable with it and developed a real affection for that big bird. In the Bible, Psalm 139:13 records a prayer of David, "For you created my inmost being; you knit me together in my mother's womb." I honestly believe today that I was born to fly. It gave me more satisfaction than just about anything in this world, other than my family.

Following training, I went to Travis as a qualified second pilot who could fly as a co-pilot in the C-124. I loved to fly that remarkable bird and when I looked at it in the National Museum of the United States Air Force recently, the sight almost brought tears to my eyes. It brought back memories of the aircraft and the professionals I flew with. Every man on every crew, pilots, navigators, loadmasters, engineers - was trained to do his job with precision. As a matter of interest, the tail number of the C-124 in the museum was 10135. I used to fly 10132 so it really seemed like the behemoth that sat there with great dignity, looming above the other displays, was an old friend.

We never stopped training. Shortly after my assignment to the 85th Air Transport Squadron, an instructor pilot and I were on a local training flight with no cargo when the instructor permitted the aircraft to demonstrate its airworthiness. First he feathered one engine. The airplane, with very little trimming, flew on with the three. Then he brought the other engine on the same side to zero power. Normally this can cause a pilot a bit of consternation, but with careful application of trim, the aircraft soldiered on. Then he brought a third engine back to zero thrust. At approximately 110,000 pounds with METO power (Maximum Except for Take Off) the aircraft, at a pressure altitude of 5,000 feet with ten degrees of flaps, would fly at 110 knots all day. The aircraft was not entirely comfortable operating with only one of four engines, but it patiently flew on, no doubt hoping that the human at the controls would soon regain his senses and restore power.

Gaining experience, I advanced to First Pilot, then later, sometime in the fall of 1957, to Aircraft Commander. Before certification as an Aircraft Commander I underwent what was called an "811 Flight". This was an examination and training flight. Examiners took two complete flight crews, including flight engineers, navigators, and others, and flew to every base to which the 85th normally flew missions. We flew all instrument approaches and had to demonstrate our proficiency at each. I happened to fly the last leg of the trip back into Travis. The examiner, Larry Ceretti, was standing up between the pilots' seats as we approached the base. He took me by surprise and asked me what our touchdown speed would be. I replied "Ninety knots," The ideal touchdown speed could vary slightly based on gross weight at landing, density altitude, and so on, and I could have made the aircraft touch down at any reasonable speed - at exactly ninety knots if I chose to. However I elected to let the wheels touch the runway at the time I felt the airplane wanted to touch down. I still remember him standing there, as he watched the airspeed indicator: "Ninety-one knots." "Ninety knots." "Eighty-nine knots." "Eighty-eight knots." "Eighty-seven God Damn knots!"

He was a perfectionist and he never asked anyone to do what he could not and would not do himself. His approach to that landing typified the precision with which our crews flew. When he and his aircraft, a C-133, later disappeared on a long flight over the Pacific, the U.S. Air Force lost a fine officer and crew.

Following the 811 flight, my next trip was as aircraft commander. In accordance with 85th policy, the right seat was occupied by another examiner, Jonathan Brown, a Captain, a fine guy and a fine pilot. Policy required that pilots have 2,000 hours and a green card (the highest instrument rating) when they became aircraft commanders. At this point, because of my combat flying in World War II and my flying in Newfoundland and at Travis, I had just reached 2,000 hours. In spite of my experience flying in the interesting weather at Northeast Air Command I had not had the opportunity to be awarded a green card.

That morning Travis was below minimums for takeoff. Captain Brown was a flight examiner, had previously given me instrument check rides, and was familiar with my work in the simulators (our simulators were bolted to the floor, but they were complete flight decks and believe me, the scenarios were very real!). He said, "You have a green card don't you?" I did not. So flight examiner Brown went to the Instrument Section where he pulled out a green card and signed it. I said, "OK, let's go". I signed as my own clearance authority and we took off.

The world was turbulent, testing of new weapons was being carried out on a remote Pacific atoll, and things were happening fast. One day, as my crew boarded the aircraft and prepared to take off on a transport mission, the flight engineer informed me that the cargo loaded by the ground crews had put the aircraft 8,000 pounds over the limit for gross takeoff weight. I called Transport Control, "Regulations do not permit me to take off." "What is your trip number?" I told him. There was a pause and then the reply came back, "You are cleared to depart over gross weight." Obviously our cargo was critical and it was urgent that we haul it without delay to where it needed to go.

MATS was never through with training. When we became certified Aircraft Commanders they still did not turn us loose to be lone wolves. For the first five or six trips the pilot in the right seat was always a flight instructor. After that we were put on our own, but in addition to flying so many hours per month we completed a quota of local training flights. The 85th Air Transport Squadron was a thoroughly professional organization.

To this day I consider it a marvelous thing that my two primary flying assignments were with such terrific organizations, staffed by men totally dedicated to their mission - the 85th and the Checkertails.

The organization had regular picnics and cookouts where officers and enlisted troops mingled freely and families attended; in a sense the 85th was one big family. It gave me great satisfaction, I must admit, when after more than one of these gatherings, my wife told me that an enlisted flight crew member had sought her out to talk to her and let her know he and a number of others respected my skill and judgment to the extent that when they saw my name on the roster they tried to get on my flight - calculating it improved to some degree the odds of returning home safely. I guess they must have felt comfortable aboard my aircraft.

C-124 in Flight

Years later, after I had completed my final overseas tour, a three year tour with the Air Weather Service in Bermuda, and was on the way to my next assignment, we traveled to Travis Air Force Base to renew acquaintances made while flying there with the 85th. I had just opened my car door and was stepping out into the afternoon sunlight when a lieutenant came running over to the car. He was a young officer who had been my co-pilot on several trans-Pacific flights and who, by chance, saw me drive up and park. The first thing he said when he ran up was, "Captain Gaston! Do you remember that landing you made at Tachi? I made one just like it!" On that particular trip he had been my first pilot when I was aircraft commander on a trip from Clark Air Force Base to Tokyo. The landing he remembered came on a leg of a multi-stop mission over the Pacific in a C-124. The C-124 "Globemaster" was an unpressurized, low altitude bird, so it was quite common to take off, fly, and land in miserable conditions - common but never routine. It was something we were trained for and expected to do.

That night, Tachi was experiencing wind, rain, fog, and minimum vertical visibility, some 200 feet and variable. Approach control gave us a clearance for the final portion of our route. He guided us in until he could hand us over to the GCA controller who watched us through our approach points on radar, and radioed to us the altitude we should be passing through at each one. Then, using standard procedure, he told us we were on glide slope, on centerline, and over the threshold.

Once we crossed the threshold, the landing was totally on my shoulders. The co-pilot said, "I have the runway visually." Now people who did not know better would look at that huge, slab sided aircraft, with its cockpit out on the front end, some thirty feet above the tarmac when the aircraft was on the ground, and tell you that the C-124 was so big its pilot surely could not possibly "feel" the airplane. He would have to do everything by the numbers. But you <u>could</u> feel it, and you needed to. That night, as always, I felt like the airplane was a part of me. As the relatively new first pilot assisted with flaps and gear, and monitored the radio, the aircraft settled gently on the runway. We reversed the props, slowed, and taxied to the parking ramp.

How gratifying it was that he remembered that night landing years later, and felt proud when he made one just like it. What a great welcome back that was! We talked a while, and I found that he was to take his line check that day to become an aircraft commander on a new bird, the C-135.

One trip stands out in my memory because of two incidents that occurred on consecutive nights in extremely bad weather. The first was on the leg of the trip where we were to land at Guam. They had just installed a GCA system and minimums had been lowered from 1200 feet to 500 feet and one mile. The runway was nestled among hills. We made our final approach to the runway on GCA in a torrential downpour and had a very strong cross wind from the left. Sparkplug problems had caused surging and backfiring necessitating shut down of one engine. Unfortunately, it was number one engine (the outboard engine on the left side) the one we really needed thrust from to control the aircrafts tendency to yaw to the left after touchdown. We located the runway at 800 feet but lost it twice on the way to touchdown. When we touched down, I started to reverse the two inboard props, but the wind was so strong and the water on the runway so deep that the aircraft hydroplaned. It was mandatory to keep it pointed straight because had the water thinned and the gear caught with the aircraft yawed to the left, it could have caused gear collapse. So I had to apply power from the inboard engine on the left side.

We were pointed down the runway but drifting sideways. The right gear dropped off the runway and I had traction for the right main gear and could slow the airplane down. At a slower speed the aircraft stopped hydroplaning and using the steerable nose wheel I could get it back on the runway. I got the aircraft stopped just as the runway end lights disappeared from view under the nose.

Oddly enough the aircraft suffered no damage, nor did I damage any runway lights with that right main gear. We taxied to the ramp and parked normally. I should note here that an Air Rescue Aircraft had come out to meet us. Supposedly, we were the first two aircraft to penetrate Hurricane Ida.

Our adventures on that trip were not over. Events that unfolded the next night highlighted the professionalism of our crews. We had departed from Agana, Guam, the scene of our hydroplaning adventure the night before, to fly to Taipei, Formosa. Our in-flight weather was no better; it was worse. Before the days of satellites, there was some uncertainty about the intensity of the weather we might encounter on those long trans-oceanic flights. We found out later that on this particular night, cruising along at 8,000 feet, we were some 200 miles from the eye of Typhoon Ida when interesting things began to happen.

Shortly after we reached cruise altitude the red warning alternator light on engine number three came on, indicating we had a hot alternator. I shut the engine down and feathered the prop. The first engineer on that flight, Master Sergeant Fort Bellringer, crawled down the long tunnel in the wing of that giant aircraft to number three engine to remove the alternator and pad the hole so the engine could be restarted. Alternator removal would have been a comparatively short job on the ground but with the aircraft pitching in the storm the job was much more difficult. While he was in the wing, engine number two began to surge and backfire. That engine had to be shut down also. We needed engine number three if we were to stay airborne without jettisoning cargo. And even if we could dump enough expensive cargo to maintain altitude, limping along on two engines at low altitude in a violent storm would not be a good situation.

Sergeant Bellringer reported that he thought the problem with the alternator was a cooling duct that had come apart. Without the ram air it was supposed to channel the alternator had overheated. I asked him if he thought he could fix it and he replied that he thought he could. He crawled back down the tunnel, reinstalled the alternator, and somehow jury-rigged the duct so the alternator would cool. Within minutes we were able to restart engine number three. It was none too soon.

I had made the decision to begin jettisoning cargo at 1500 feet. On two engines, unable to maintain altitude, the aircraft had descended from 8,000 feet down to 1800 feet when we were able to restart engine number three and slowly begin to regain some altitude. I was proud of the way every member of my crew performed that night. Jettisoning cargo is a touchy operation under the best of conditions because the center of gravity of the aircraft cannot be thrown too far off. In the turbulent air of that storm, limping along on two engines, the operation would have become even more difficult. Yet the Loadmaster, Staff Sergeant Theodore Smith, had performed the necessary calculations and had the cargo in position. My first pilot, Lieutenant George Garcia, did his job flawlessly, assisting with the aircraft which was pitching violently in the storm and communicating with Guam Air Traffic Control and the Air Rescue Service. I knew that my decisions had to be correct and that I had to remain cool. The situation was challenging, but it was the kind of thing MATS trained its pilots for.

I elected to land at Anderson Air Force Base on Guam, rather than return to Agana because it was closer, it had longer, wider runways, and there was a possibility of slightly better weather with less turbulence. As we approached Guam, the same Air Rescue Aircraft came out to meet us. The pilot radioed, "Didn't I just talk to you recently?" "As a matter of fact you did; we've got to quit meeting like this!"

Every member of the crew contributed to our safe landing that night. The Assistant Engineer, Staff Sergeant Robert Proano took over the engineer's panel while Sergeant Bellringer was in the wing, monitoring and reporting engine status. The Navigator, Lieutenant Harold Katzman, who was receiving his initial line check on that flight, did his job in a manner that would have been a credit to a far more experienced man. He provided me with up to date position reports, distances back to Guam, and ETAs at possible landing sites. After we landed, during the remainder of the night, my engineers supervised the maintenance of the aircraft, Sergeant Smith repositioned the cargo, and we were on our way before noon the next day.

I guess you could say the fun wasn't over on that trip. We continued on to Taipei, Formosa. We were cruising along over the open sea when all at once a C-124 emerged from a cumulus in front of us. I had to take evasive action to avoid hitting it broadside. I don't think the pilot even saw us. We landed at Formosa, unloaded, and refueled. I felt the crew needed rest and made the decision to stay overnight. "No, you can't do that!" It was 1958 and tensions between the Chinese communists and the Nationalists were high. "It is not safe to leave that aircraft on the ground here overnight." So we took off again, this time for Okinawa. The weather continued violent; thunderstorms were everywhere. St. Elmo's fire was so bright you could have read a newspaper in the cockpit. The navigator reported that communications were totally disrupted by the storms and he could not get a fix. I told him to give me a heading to Okinawa and then get on the radar and steer me between cells. He did and when we broke out, it was like going through a door into the clear, and there was Okinawa dead ahead about seventy miles.

On the next leg of that trip, going to Guam, we had another hot generator. We had no cargo by now. We feathered the engine and flew on. Captain Garcia was in the left seat. He asked, "Do you want me to move over and give you this seat?" I told him no, that I had confidence in him. He flew on in and landed with three engines. He was an excellent pilot.

When I returned from a subsequent trip, I was surprised to learn that an account of the incident had appeared in the local newspaper. Major Robert Bleier, the flight examiner who had joined us to conduct Lieutenant Katzman's line check, had provided the story to the local newspaper. Lieutenant Katzman passed his line check with flying colors.

Someone saw that story and called our house and asked my wife, "Is this the John Gaston who served in the 325th Fighter Group in Italy?" It turned out to be my crew chief from the 325th, Clifton P. (Pat) Patterson. What a reunion that was! Pat was a dock chief at Travis, directing maintenance on the birds I flew.

A young officer who flew with me had grown up in Norway, and was a boy of nine or ten when the Germans moved in and occupied Norway. On one flight he described that experience in vivid detail. Norway had complete gun registration. When the Nazis rolled their trucks full of soldiers into town they went straight to the City Hall and seized the records that showed every gun owner and the firearms he owned. The Germans then posted a notice saying that every firearm was to be turned in immediately to the occupying army. Some Norwegians complied, some did not. For those that did not, the German army had a quick response. Soldiers went to the offender's house, dragged the non-complying gun owner out, and executed him on the spot. I will never forget what my young co-pilot said that day when he told me the story. "John, don't ever let them make you register your guns!"

Because the C-124 was not pressurized for high altitude flight, our trips were always made at much lower altitudes than trans-oceanic flights are made today. We could not fly above the weather. I remember one particular trip because of a comment my copilot made. We were flying aircraft number 10132 at an assigned altitude of 9,000 feet, heavily loaded with fuel, on the way to Wake Island from Tokyo.

Only in an emergency would a deliberate departure from an assigned altitude be carried out, and then only after contact with IFR traffic control at the location assigned responsibility for the sector in which an aircraft was operating. We encountered heavy weather with pronounced turbulence. Updrafts and downdrafts occasioned by thunderstorms would carry us rapidly up as much as a thousand feet above our assigned altitude or drop us a thousand feet below it. Fortunately, from the standpoint of avoiding other traffic, one could assume that any aircraft assigned an altitude a thousand feet below us, or a thousand feet above us, would be experiencing the same roller coaster ride, and safe separation would be maintained. I was busy keeping the aircraft in an even attitude and almost immediately occupied with a more severe problem. Sudden and severe icing, perhaps from supersaturated air in the thunderstorms, began to build up on the aircraft. Icing, of course, can disrupt the airflow over an airfoil, so it threatens both the efficiency of the propellers and the lift offered by the wings. The C-124 was equipped with electric heaters for the propeller blades and had on each wing tip a gasoline heater which supplied heated air to the wind leading edge and part of the upper surface. A third gasoline heater supplied hot air to the tail surfaces, so at least for the time being, thrust was maintained and the aircraft could maintain altitude.

There was nothing to do but obey what many instructors might refer to as the prime directive of pilotage: First, fly the airplane. In the midst of this wild rock and roll ride the navigator reported all communication with the outside world had been lost. Ice had stripped the aircraft of all its wire antennas; only the stubs remained. It had lost two trailing wire antennas and when he asked if he should let out the third - the last available - I told him to wait until we broke out of the storms, because we would absolutely need it then to reestablish contact with land.

Eventually, after a seemingly endless time, we did break out into the clear. In the middle of it all however, the copilot was getting airsick. Not wanting the results of airsickness splashed all over the flight deck I suggested it might be prudent for him to get up, go back, and lie down on a cot for a few minutes. He complied, but when he had climbed out of his seat, he put his hand on my shoulder and paid me what I considered a high compliment, "You son-of-a-bitch. You're enjoying this!"

At a point midway in my tour I had been recommended for the rating of Instructor Pilot but was turned down by the board because I did not have enough time in the C-124, only about 400 hours. Not long afterward, recommended once more, I was designated an instructor pilot, to my knowledge, with the lowest aircraft time in the one twenty four of anyone appointed up to that point. I had something like 600 hours in the aircraft.

The time drew near when my tour with the 85th Air Transport Squadron was scheduled to end. Air Weather Service was insisting I be returned to them. The Chief Pilot in the 85th gave me a line check. When we got back he said, "Well John, we're going to designate some more flight examiners and you are to be put on the list to be advanced to flight examiner. It is important that you know how highly we think of you. In spite of the fact that you are leaving, we will do this." Momentarily, I was overcome and could not answer, but then I realized it would serve no practical purpose for the organization and there was little probability, once I left, that I would ever fly a C-124 again. I told him that and how much I appreciated the honor (To my knowledge I would have been a flight examiner with one of the very lowest total hours in the C-124 in the Pacific Division) but it was enough for me to know that the organization would be willing to do that. He said, "OK".

At that time I was told that if I wanted to remain and fly, the 85th would, and could, see to it that it would come about. Although this was my deepest desire, there were compelling personal reasons involving my family for me to leave that flying duty. For one, my wife did not like my constant trips across the Pacific. There was a meaningful accident toll and she had become increasingly uneasy each time I departed on a mission. I could not continue flying the C-124, although I very much wanted to, but I had the satisfaction of knowing that it was something I could do.

As it turned out, it was the right decision. Had I stayed, I know that things at home would not have worked out too well. I chose overseas again and was fortunate to be assigned a three year tour in Bermuda, January 1959 through 1962, something that, in part because of the friendships she made there, was the best thing I could have done for my daughter.

In January 1962 I was ordered back to the States and assigned to NORAD (the North American Air Defense Command). I was able to fly there too, to various destinations, and often made trips from Colorado Springs to Andrews and back. On one such trip in a C-54, we had a scheduled stop at Wright Patterson Air Force Base near Dayton, Ohio. My younger brother who was stationed there at the time, with his wife, brought their two small boys out to see their uncle. Afterward, the younger, who was perhaps two years old at the time, would hold up four fingers and proudly say, "Uncle John's airplane has this much pellers."

Preparing for a flight as copilot one stormy morning in Colorado Springs, I asked the aircraft commander what the minimums were for takeoff. He said, "Well, we have two." "First, can you find the airplane?" "Then, can you find the runway?"

I was assigned to the 4th Weather Wing in support of NORAD. There I served as Weather Officer and staff briefer. (Life Magazine at that time published a picture taken from the back of the auditorium of a group being briefed in the NORAD center. Way up on the stage, so small in the picture you would not recognize who it was unless you knew beforehand, there I was, delivering my weather briefing.) I retired from that assignment effective 1 May 1965. Thirty April was my last day to wear the uniform of the U.S. Air Force on active duty.

Chapter Five: Corporate Pilot

"Why don't you just come up and fly our airplane." Those words were like a ray of sunshine breaking through heavy clouds on a gray day. Those words were spoken - that question asked - by the chief engineer of Plateau Natural Gas Company in casual conversation following a wedding ceremony we attended in Colorado Springs in 1966. To a man who had shortly before left a career spanning more than two decades in the Army Air Corps and U.S. Air Force only to find that a new career selling life insurance did not offer the bright prospects he had expected, they were welcome words.

As a casualty assistance officer after World War II, I was given two file cabinets stuffed with file folders; each file folder represented a service man who had been killed or was listed as missing in action. My area of responsibility included all of the State of Michigan, Northeast Indiana, and Northwest Ohio. I was given a staff car and a driver and covered many miles of road in that area.

I had come to appreciate the value of life insurance to survivors of military men who had lost their lives in the service of their country, and, by extension, the value that life insurance could have for survivors of other breadwinners. I had come to believe that life insurance should have a place in the budget of every household. I hoped that, eventually when I retired, I could make a reasonable living as a life insurance underwriter. On a very limited basis I had sold insurance part-time during part of my career and viewed what I did as a service. I certainly did not make much money at it, but thought it a worthwhile thing to do.

The customary sales practices employed by other sales personnel did not always fit with my sense of ethics. My company was a reputable company (I would not have gone to work for one that was not) but company personnel who discussed prospective levels of income I could be expected to earn said very little about sales practices. No doubt they assumed such discussions could come later – or perhaps they were not accustomed to dealing with an individual raised by highly ethical parents in a rural Kansas environment where honesty and honor were highly valued. I chose not to follow all the customary sales practices and apparently that is why my sales levels, and income, did not match what I anticipated they would be. In short I needed to find another job to feed my family and I needed to find that job without delay.

While I was still on active duty and living in Colorado Springs, a new neighbor moved in next door. It happened that he was the chief engineer for Plateau Natural Gas Company. He knew from chance conversations that I was a ham radio operator and had once been a communications officer. One day he came over and asked if I could possibly install a part in their chart reading machine. I replied that I would need to take a look at it but probably could do so. We drove to the office and I installed the part.

When I had retired my wife and I had moved to Albuquerque (where I had gone into the insurance business). A short time later we drove back to Colorado Springs to attend a wedding; the daughter of an old friend I had known on active duty was getting married. The engineer also attended. He and I were talking after the ceremony when he asked, "Are you doing well there in Albuquerque?" I replied honestly, "No." "I'm looking for another job." That was when he said the magic words, "Why don't you come up to Colorado Springs and fly our airplane?" I said, "That sounds good to me. What kind of equipment do you have?" The next day we were still in Colorado Springs, visiting friends, when he called: "Can you come down for an interview?" "You bet!"

They set up an interview for that day and I was interviewed by the vice president for operations, Charles McGee, who gave me an application for employment and requested that I take it home, fill it out, and return it to them. When I returned to Albuquerque I did so without delay. They telephoned me and wanted to know if I could come back for another interview. Again I said, "You bet!"

So we set a date and this time I was interviewed by the president of the company, Bruce Fullerton, the vice president for operations, Charles McGee, and another executive of the company Stan Jervis. We set in Bruce's office and talked for close to an hour. Then Stan Jarvis got up and left the room. When he returned he gave me a couple of keys; they were the keys to their airplane. And that's how I became an employee of Plateau Natural Gas Company.

My first day of employment was 10 October 1966. There was a great deal of discussion and a general information exchange about where I would fit in the company but the first item on the agenda was to get checked out in the airplane. I did this with one of the fixed base operators at Peterson Field who was both an instructor pilot and flight examiner and totally familiar with the Cessna 310 the company operated. When he was satisfied that I was checked out, they set up a weeklong training program in Dallas, Texas, at Love Field with a company called Flight Proficiency.

It was a good school. They had a ground school and several link trainers, and of course instructors who flew with you every day during that week. Mine was a Cuban with an excellent background who had successfully escaped from Cuba. At the end of that week if they figured you were ready they passed you on to a flight examiner who gave a very comprehensive instrument check. The day came when I was scheduled for that flight and I was drinking a cup of hot chocolate in the lobby there and this examiner walked up to me and identified himself "My name is Slick Slaughter." I just turned around and headed in the other direction. Slaughter got quite a kick out of that. Then we went out to the airplane, did the walk around, the run-up, and he gave me a list of things he wanted me to do. We took off and I must say it was a real comprehensive check ride. When we came back in he said, "Well, I guess you can go ahead and fly your people around." The next day I returned to Colorado Springs.

Plateau was a special company and it was the ideal company for me. Back on the farm we were a 'family'. How to define that? We cared for each other, we knew if we didn't carry our share of the load someone else would have to pick up the slack. All of us were raised with the knowledge that we had an obligation to help one another when we could. Growing up, I was expected, as were my brothers and sisters, to exercise initiative and get things done. We were taught to ask ourselves "What task needs to be done to get the corn planted, the chores done, the hay in the stack, whatever. . . ?"

The managers of Plateau had built a company with a team spirit where initiative was encouraged. I suppose you could say the company was to some extent run on a shoestring and consequently the pay was not as high as it might have been in a big corporation, but it seemed fair to me and the company was blissfully free of bureaucratic rules. That environment gave me the freedom to try new things, learn more about how the company worked, and to contribute in any area I could.

After flying for three or four weeks I went into Bruce Fullerton's office and I said to him, "Flying this airplane is not going to fill all my time and while I have no problem flying the airplane I know nothing about the gas business and would like to learn something." He was favorably impressed with this and said, "OK. We'll see to it."

I was an experienced weather forecaster. I updated their climatological data on the stations they served and revised their degree day forecasting, all very important for predicting peak demand, to contract for gas to be delivered. Extra gas half way though winter? Costs more to get. Accurate forecasts were important for the bottom line. This led to a number of things concerned with meteorology. Bruce called me into his office. "You're an old farm boy. I want you to be our liaison with county extension agents in our service area and in addition the agricultural department guys up at Fort Collins." In addition to that I was to be the company representative at the South East Colorado Economic Development District.

The next thing I got into built on my background as a communications and electronics officer in the service. I was put in charge of the company's communication system which had been set up to tie together pipelines and pumping systems scattered throughout Western Kansas, Northwest Texas, and Eastern Colorado. It included 150 mobile units and 16 base stations scattered over this vast territory. I became involved in antenna leasing agreements, and later, working closely with engineers from Motorola from whom we bought our communications equipment, designed antennas to reach into the mountainous regions of Southwest Colorado in the Durango-Gunnison area.

Some three years later Bruce walked into my office. Two men from E. F. Hutton had flown out to Colorado Springs to examine Plateau because its owner-managers were thinking of going public. "What I want you to do is put these two guys in the airplane , fly around the whole system, visit some locations, explain what we have, answer any questions they have." I thought, "He is putting the whole company right in my hands!" Yes, I had been involved in many areas and probably knew as much about the operations of the business as any single person. He didn't get the engineer or the treasurer, he got the airplane driver. I did as directed. Company management later changed their mind and decided to sell out instead.

Plateau was very customer - oriented. An example was the work it did with a drilling engineer from Nebraska, whose idea was to get the maximum bang out of the buck that farmers spent for fuel to irrigate their crops. Plateau was in the natural gas business but to quite an extent you could say we got into the irrigation business. We wanted to do analysis that would allow us to make forecasts in our service regions concerning the acre-inches of water that would be needed at various times of the year and how much natural gas it would take to pump this water. This kind of analysis required liaison not only with the Colorado water people but also the Kansas water people in Topeka. The objective was to match pumps to wells for the irrigation system in use, and in turn this was linked to the crops they needed to raise - with the objective of minimizing water usage and fuel use consistent with what the crops needed. Well capacity would dictate what water could be pumped in a given period, as needed by various crops, and this called for particular pumps, and engines for those pumps fueled by our natural gas

At about this time the Gates Rubber Company decided to get into corporate farm activity in Northeast Colorado where they were leasing land. This would require irrigation of extensive new acreage and we had very few pipelines into that area. This meant several things: we needed to know what they wanted to grow, we needed to estimate how much water that would take, determine what the aquifer under the land would produce, and how many wells could be legally drilled. This, in turn, would determine how much natural gas we needed to supply and would be the basis for designing the pipeline system that we would need to install, including compression facilities. It was a complicated and involved process. A process I was very much involved in. It was a learning experience and I thrived on it. I had to learn a great deal about aquifers - porosity, capacity, the velocity with which the water flowed through them, and a number of other things.

Another thing we were trying to integrate into these calculations was probable rainfall. Here my meteorological background was of value. I had approximately 100 rain gauges that were given to farmers, district managers, and others throughout the area that Plateau served. We were trying to determine if we could come up with any information on rainfall patterns that we could use to make our operation more efficient. It was unfortunate that we did not get to finish that particular project. It was interrupted when we were purchased by a larger gas company Northern Natural Gas Company. Plateau was merged into what was called Peoples Natural Gas, the distribution arm of Northern Natural Gas.

All along I continued to fly the airplane on company business throughout our service area. This involved taking care of hangar space, meeting maintenance requirements, and all the myriad of things that go along with a small aviation operation, including my own training.

When we were purchased by Northern Natural Gas and merged into the Peoples Division, their employee relations people came down to update what they considered our somewhat primitive organizational structure. One of the first things they wanted to accomplish was to prepare formal job descriptions for all employees. They came to my desk, for example, gave me a pad, and said, "Please write down the things that you do." So I wrote down a list of all the things that I was busily involved in from day to day. When they read through my list their response was a somewhat - horrified, "We can't write a job description like this!" "Why not?" "It covers too many different skill lines of work!" How could reality be crammed into a textbook formal job description? They finally figured it out. According to official company policies, they said, "What we really need down here is an Employee-Relations and District Safety Administrator!" So now I had two new jobs. The other things that I did they lumped into a phrase "... And other assignments and duties that the regional vice president may direct." That included flying and all the other things I was doing.

After a few months the parent company decided that we could not, as a region of the company, own our own aircraft because the parent company, Northern Natural Gas, already had an "Aviation Department" and several airplanes. So our airplane was sold at a bargain basement price to a convenient buyer. They said, "We have nothing against you flying but you cannot, according to company policy, <u>own</u> an airplane." There are times when company policy is one thing and efficiency and cost minimization are something else entirely. Our executives still needed to visit various parts of the system and other company business justified use of an aircraft. The aircraft we had owned had been extremely useful in multiple roles. We had to rent an airplane when needed, on a trip basis, and, since the parent company desired that we should have two pilots instead of just me, we not only had to rent an airplane but a pilot as well. This made the cost of the aviation department and its contribution to overhead significantly larger than it had been before. This arrangement continued however for another four or five years.

During that period, in conjunction with district managers and others, I established a training program that resulted in getting thirteen of our personnel qualified in first aid instruction. We then conducted first aid training throughout our service region. I conducted a number of these training sessions myself. During that time we qualified well over 1,000 people in first aid, concentrating on school bus drivers, law enforcement people, teachers, and other citizens who were interested. I had taken the idea to Bruce Fullerton, he approved of it, and the company received a tremendous amount of good will in the communities we served.

During this period I also flew with the Northern Natural Gas aviation department as a crew member in their Cessna 421s. They were pressurized and had greater power, a higher ceiling, and other nice to have features not possessed by our Cessna 310. Their chief pilot would come down to Colorado Springs and give regular proficiency checks in the 421 just as was done for personnel assigned to the aviation department at home base in Omaha.

As a part of my employee relations duties I wrote many job descriptions, became involved with payroll and payroll budgeting, and was assigned to distribute and present lectures on company benefit plans. These included the medical plan, the retirement plan, and the savings plans that they had for employees.

It was in this capacity that I was able to step into the breach and save an employee's job. In one of our districts there was an employee who was a controlled epileptic. While on a company-sanctioned coffee break he had a seizure. While this would likely not happen today, at that time my younger and somewhat impatient supervisor, who had been sent down to Plateau by Peoples, basically wanted to get rid of the guy. I said, "No." It turned out that the man had gone to his doctor to get a prescription renewed and found the doctor had gone on vacation. He had been seen by another doctor who changed his prescription. I discussed the employee with four district supervisors who were familiar with the guys work, and with his regular doctor who had returned from vacation and suggested that the employee might well be transferred to duties were his handicap would not be hazardous to himself or others around him. A transfer was arranged to the meter maintenance shop in that region and the employee did very well there, until one day when an unfortunate incident occurred. Men were grouped together waiting for paychecks to be handed out when someone behind this individual "goosed" him sharply in the ribs. In a flash the offending man was lying on the floor. The individual in question, instinctively, had decked him. According to policy that was grounds for dismissal. Once again I went to bat for the guy and he was transferred to another region where he was a model employee. His job was saved, his family continued to eat regularly, and the company retained a valuable, dedicated employee.

There was another incident in the benefits arena involving a young employee whose wife had a problem pregnancy and severe health problems for some time afterward, resulting in very high medical bills. His claims for reimbursement under the health plan were denied. When I looked into the circumstances it was very clear to me that an injustice was being done. When this employee was hired, some of the paper work concerning the medical plan was incomplete. Certain forms were not included. I did not hesitate but took the matter to our corporate benefits department, "This is not fair treatment of our employee!" They agreed, and the employee was fully reimbursed. He was extremely grateful and became a long-time, valued employee.

Plateau was not only customer oriented - the company was employee oriented - another reason that I admired our Colorado Springs managers and received a great deal of satisfaction from working there.

About this time, as companies frequently do, they decided to reorganize. They decided to eliminate the office of the Western region. People were to be either laid off or given the opportunity to transfer to the Omaha - Council Bluffs area. People's Division was located across the river from Omaha, at Council Bluffs, Iowa. I still needed a job of course and expected a transfer. I still do not know why, but for a long time I was not told whether I would have a job at People's or not. This caused concern on my part and on the part of my family. Finally they said, "We have picked you to be director of safety for the whole of People's." I accepted. After we moved I learned that the aviation department wanted a replacement for their dispatcher, who was planning retirement. I discussed this opening and my qualifications for it with the man who was to be my supervisor at People's, and he gave me the go-ahead to apply for the aviation position. Out of some 40 applications for the job mine was chosen and I was hired. This transferred me out of the Peoples Division to the aviation department of the parent corporation, Northern Natural Gas Company.

At that time it was evident that there was not enough depth in the aviation department. For example, had something happened to the manager, there was no one trained to take his place. Company management became aware of this situation and, in a very few months, rewrote the job description for the dispatcher. I became assistant to the manager of the aviation department. This worked out well, they decided to expand my duties, and I became a crew member for the right seat of the Cessna Citation. I was sent to Dallas to the school American Airlines ran for Cessna Citation people. I didn't get a lot of flying time in the citation at that time, but with personnel changes and retirements they soon needed more depth in their Saber Liner crew roster. So I was sent to Flight Safety International at St. Louis for training in the Saber Liner. The North American Saber Liner was a fine airplane. Its design had been derived in part from experience its manufacturer had gained in design and production of the superb F-86 Fighter that had earned a distinguished record in the Korean War. Apparently many of the engineers and designers of the Saber Liner had been involved with that excellent aircraft.

It was at about this time that the company decided to purchase a Desault Falcon 50 and they needed to train an additional crewmember after it was delivered. As it happened I was on a trip and sitting in an airport in New Jersey when I was directed to go to Teterboro in New Jersey to Flight Safety International and attend ground school on this fantastic aircraft. This also included some flight instruction. A pilot named Don Foreman, an excellent pilot who had been with the company for many years, received more flight instruction because he was to become a Captain on the falcon. I was destined to remain First Officer or copilot.

Because of his ability I think Don was an excellent choice to be aircraft captain on the Falcon. However, this does bring up the scheme under which the aviation department determined eligibility for promotion to aircraft captain. It mattered not how many hours of flight time a pilot had outside the company, or the variety and depth of his experience flying different types of aircraft. All that counted was seniority - years of service with the aviation department. At that time I had more than 5,000 logged hours in a variety of aircraft ranging from high-performance fighters to the largest, long-range transport of its time. That counted for nothing. In accordance with company policy, for example, they might well have hired a pilot from outside the company with only four hundred hours but if he had come into the aviation department a month earlier than I did he would be in line to advance to Captain before I would, in whatever aircraft he was flying.

It became increasingly obvious that a number of people in the aviation department, for whatever reason, resented the presence of former military pilots. Someone at the company asked me one day (perhaps trying to get a rise out of me) if this seniority rule did not bother me. My reply? "Not really." I had been an international aircraft captain twenty years before. "My experience has been that the right seat arrives at any given destination at the same time the left seat does. And my job is to do all I can to ensure that both seats arrive safely." As they say, I knew I had already, "Been there and done that" and I did not feel I had anything to prove, in terms of status, in that rather small and confined aviation organization.

The company at that time had three variants of the Saber Liner, a Citation, and the Falcon 50. Normally pilots were only approved to fly two of these five aircraft, however, when a new captain was promoted – just by accident of scheduling of course – I was often scheduled to ride the right seat with them until they became more familiar with the airplane. I often had more time in each of these airplanes then a newly appointed captain did when they were promoted. One day I asked the manager of the aviation department why there was a two airplane limitation on all the other pilots and yet I flew all five. Silence ensued. Then after a long pause, as if he didn't really know what to say, he said simply, "You're different."

The Falcon 50

While there seemed to be an undercurrent of – what should we call it? Animosity? Envy? It's hard to define exactly – among the majority of the flying personnel in the aviation department, such did not exist with our excellent maintenance people. They consistently did an excellent job and kept our small fleet in top condition. I recognized that fact and they knew it. We had an excellent working relationship.

In addition to the fact that I was a former military pilot I found there was another bone of contention – my meteorological background. Captains made go-no go decisions on any flight. It was made plain to me that, as a copilot, I was not to influence the captain's decision at any time in this regard. I was accused of doing that one time – and the only proof I had that I had not done so was that the particular captain stated that I had not. The captain was a pilot whose services had been contracted from outside the company and the aircraft had been rented because of scheduling problems. That day it was raining hard; the weather was not good. That individual did not have transportation so I offered to drive him up to flight services were he could check the weather. We drove up there. I said nothing and let him make the decision. As we drove back to the organization his demeanor was very serious. Reaching a decision, when we arrived he said "I'm not going to go." It didn't matter what I said after that, I was branded as the presumptuous guy who influenced a captain's go-no go decision. And that's the way it was.

Following that incident, relationships within the aviation department became more difficult. Interestingly enough, it was very apparent that executives in the Northern Natural Gas Company felt that I was doing my job well. There were 15 or 16 top people in the organization who could levy the aviation department for trips. Each of these executives had a highly efficient secretary who arranged his detailed calendar and took care of travel arrangements. It was after I had worked closely with all of these people for some five years that the executive secretaries got together in a group and, shortly before my retirement, took my wife and me to lunch one day – a definite compliment because it had never happened before in the history of that organization.

Eventually, responsibilities regarding my extended family made it apparent that I should elect to retire (my brother was ill and his affairs needed oversight and my wife's mother had grown unable to take care of herself alone down in Sweetwater, Texas). When I did, another event occurred that stands out as a highlight of my period of employment in the aviation department at People's Natural Gas. The executive secretaries, one of whom worked directly for the president of the corporation, again as a group, arranged a retirement party and ceremony for me, to which my wife of course was invited, along with any other company personnel who knew me and might wish to say goodbye. A number of top-level executives from Northern attended - some of them men who had come over from Plateau. Over 100 people signed the guest book. The manager of the aviation department and the chief pilot made a very brief, perfunctory appearance because it was obviously mandatory. Not one other person from the aviation department - many of whom I had flown on trips with, here there and everywhere - attended.

It was about this time that a decision had been made - as I understood it - to merge with a pipeline company in Texas called Houston Natural Gas Company. As a part of my duties as a corporate pilot ferrying our Northern Natural Gas Company executives to various meetings and discussions, I got to know many of them very well and admired them for both their intelligence and their integrity. I also had a somewhat limited opportunity to be around a few executives of the company that was to be part of the merger.

In accordance with corporate policy, prior to my retirement, I was given the choice of taking the value of my accrued retirement in the form of an annuity contract with a reputable insurance company, or conversion of my vested sum into corporate stock in the company. That corporate stock would of course have been stock in the combined company. I elected to take the paid up commercial insurance annuity.

There was one pilot in the aviation department that I had some degree of friendship with, and when I was in his area some time later, I called his house, and went out to visit him, now very ill and retired. He told me a story that was heartbreaking. "John" he said, "Two years ago my retirement fund" (in stock of the combined company) "was valued at well over two million dollars. Today it is practically worthless. All my wife and I have is our Social Security." The name of the corporation that came from the merger? Enron.

Chapter Six: Brother Buck

If you ever pick up a Louis L'Amour novel that features a character named "William Tell Sackett" you may see him described as, "still having the bark on." In many ways my older brother was like that. He was brave, hard working, and could be as tough in interpersonal relationships as a situation might require. Much like our father, he was also extremely intelligent, intensely loyal, and a man who could do just about anything he set out to do. He also had a kind streak and the ability to smoothly fit into almost any social situation. He was the kind of man I wanted to grow up to be.

When our grandfather passed away, I was seven, Robert was 13. From that time on, he carried an increasing share of the work on our dustbowl-era Kansas farm. The eldest son, he was our father's strong right hand man, even as a teen ager. Mother called him "Sonny Boy" and I don't remember when I started calling him 'Buck'. I think the name must have come from some of the other young men he associated with. He was widely respected. When neighboring farmers wanted someone to help drive tractor, harvest, or run a combine they sought him out. (Combines were very new then, and expensive - and few farmers could afford them.) He was hired his last full summer at home to drive a combine and follow the wheat harvest north as it ripened. The owner of that rare and expensive implement had entrusted its operation to Buck.

Our dry-land farm (and it <u>was</u> very dry in the thirties) was something over 120 acres. Our grandfather had purchased it sometime in the 1880s. We had another 80 acres approximately a half mile to the west we called, naturally enough, the "west eighty". Because of the sparse pasture and the fact that most of the farm, except for hay, was planted to corn. Wheat, or oats, in the hope there would be enough rain for a crop, our few cows had to be kept at the West Eighty most of the spring, summer, and fall. There was no well there, only an intermittent creek that ran briefly in the spring and then dried up. Robert would get up in the predawn darkness, put our only saddle on his horse's back, ride to that pasture, and drive the cows to the home place. He, my father, and I would pump water with a hand pump to water them. In the drier months we would often pump that well dry and then have to drive the cows on an eighth of a mile or so north. There, in the bottom of a draw, was a second well with a hand pump. There were occasions when we pumped it dry also.

Once they were milked, the cows had to be driven back to the dry pasture. In addition of course Buck helped with planting and harvesting and repairing of fence and buildings. When a crop of wheat or oats was ready to cut, Daddy had what was called a "grain binder" which cut the stalks and carried them by means of an endless canvas to a mechanism that bundled them and tied them with twine and then dropped the bundles in the field. My sisters helped with "shocking" the bundles, grain end up off the ground, and a bundle laid across the top for some limited rain deflection. Almost all the farmers followed this same procedure, and when an operator arrived in the area towing a giant threshing machine he would go from farm to farm and all the farmers around would gather with teams and wagons to haul loads of bundles to feed the monster that separated the grain and blew the straw into giant piles.

Buck always had a trap line out in winter and sold hides for the few pennies they would bring. If a neighbor had a job to do that was considered particularly responsible, such as driving one of the rare tractors a few farmers used instead of horses, they sought out my brother to work for them. Crops were scant, prices were depressed, and the family needed every penny he could earn and he did his part.

How Robert ever found time to study I do not know, yet he was an excellent student. One year, in a geometry test administered across Kansas, he was awarded a gold medal for achieving number one rank in the state. Today, that kind of ability would bring college scholarship offers flooding in, but not in those days. We lived almost a hundred miles from any college, and there was no money. The Dust Bowl and

Great Depression both were realities of life, realities that severely limited our options.

After he graduated from high school, in the summer before my senior year, we heard of an opportunity to work on the railroad. The Union Pacific was hiring men for an "extra gang" to repair flood damage to the right of way near Marysville, the county seat. We applied for work, and being strong farm boys we were hired. I was seventeen but told them I was eighteen to get the job. Our family needed the money.

Robert had agreed to run a combine that summer but stayed on the extra gang for three weeks to be sure his little brother could survive among a group of very rough and tough men. When three weeks were up and he had assured himself that I could hold my own in that company, he left and kept his promise to drive combine through the wheat harvest. To have him there the first few weeks was a real comfort. To my good fortune I was befriended by an older man who had traveled up and down the railroad doing manual labor and who seemingly had friends in every town of any size. Perhaps some of them were fences, I do not know, certainly some of the men had business associates in that line of work. I still remember him telling me something like, "Now if you are stranded in Kansas City, this is the guy to see, and in Topeka someone else. But stay away from (some establishments, and certain areas)."

Robert picked up most of my share of the work when I was in high school and that made it possible for me to letter in football, basketball, and track all four years. He rejoiced in my achievement.

When war came he was one of the first drafted from our area. He went through basic training and was assigned to the Coast Artillery someplace in California. He applied for aviation cadets, probably when inducted, took the required exams, and brilliant man that he was, passed them with flying colors. He was ordered into the aviation cadet program, earned his silver wings and commission, and was designated as a multi-engine bomber pilot.

While still in the Coast Artillery he had quickly been made a corporal or buck sergeant. He sent our father one of more copies of the post newspaper. It was called the "Ozlefinch" - however it was spelled. There was a mood of panic in the air; the country feared that the Japanese strike on Pearl Harbor might be followed by an invasion on the West Coast. At this time he was given responsibility for a small group ordered to set up a machine gun covering a designated section of beach along a lonely stretch of the California Coast. They were told that there was no activity permitted in the area and to assume that any suspicious activity was part of an invasion.

There was some moonlight, and far out on the water the nervous G.I.s made out some sort of craft. Quickly he got on the field telephone. "We have observed craft out on the water." "There is nobody on the water tonight." "But we see something." "Impossible." The seconds ticked off. "Boats are coming ashore. Are you sure there is no activity scheduled?" "No." "None!" He had no choice but to order the crew to open fire and was ready when a panicked voice came over the phone, "Hold your fire! We just got word. They told no one but the marines are practicing a night landing on that beach!"

Buck completed the rigorous program of aviation flight training in Class 43-G and was assigned as co-pilot on a B-24 four engine bomber. Often offered the opportunity to move to the left seat with his own crew, he always turned that opportunity down. His crew, to the last man, had agreed that each would do his best to improve the odds of their survival. At night, when their contemporaries were taking their mind off their rigorous training with some diversion, their crew, both officers and the enlisted men who would man the guns, would go to the hanger, board a B-24, and prepare for war. They reached the point where every man could field strip the machine guns in the dark and handle emergency situations they could anticipate.

Robert may have been the bravest man I ever knew. Like many other Liberator crews, they sometimes returned home with one or even two engines out (The aircraft, if not too badly damaged, would limp along on two engines if empty of bombs and with everything not bolted down thrown overboard) and frequently with holes in their airplane. He told me that after one landing at their home field he felt a lump behind his back. He reached back and found a chuck of flak, "big enough to hold in your hand" lodged in his flight jacket. I am in awe of the bravery his crew and others like them showed, holding steady on their bomb runs, while flak burst all around them and sometimes destroyed aircraft beside them.

I think one incident well describes the bravery and coolness under fire that he showed. They were returning from a mission where anti-aircraft fire had been particularly wicked. Many systems on their B-24 were no longer operating, including the fuel transfer system needed to route fuel to their remaining engines if they were to make it out of enemy territory. The inoperative system of fuel transfer valves was located in the bomb bay area. Critical hydraulic systems were out, so the bomb bay doors could not be shut, and they hung open in the 150-200 mile per hour wind stream. Their only hope would involve someone going out on the narrow catwalk down the middle of the bomb bay, precariously perched above the open doors, to see if it was possible to manually operate the system to transfer the fuel.

Some peculiarity of the aircraft structure, empty bomb racks perhaps, I do not know, made it impossible to reach that spot wearing a parachute. Buck removed his chute, leaving it in the cockpit, and went out on that catwalk in the roaring wind. They were still at altitude, so it was quite cold and the wind swirling around from the open bomb bay doors must have made it difficult to avoid falling and being swept out those gaping open doors. I don't know how long he was out there but he managed to hold on with one hand and manipulate the valve controls with the other so the vital fuel was transferred. When finished, he made his way back to the cockpit, donned his chute - no doubt with frozen hands - and they made it to base.

On paper, the B-24 Liberator was, one might say, marginally superior to the B-17 in range, payload, and speed. But critics insisted it did not possess the ruggedness of the fabled B-17 Flying Fortress and dubbed it the "Flying Coffin". My brother had another close brush with death the day I flew a Mustang fresh out of the shop on a test hop to his base. There I found, of seven B-24s in good repair the squadron had managed to put in the air and send out on a mission that day, only two made it back. As recounted earlier, three were destroyed; his was one of two that made it to an island held at that time by Yugoslav Partisans.

I do not doubt that it was the Hand of Providence that brought that crew through thirty five missions and returned it home. Buck was a battle-hardened veteran and his experience and ability were quickly put to use. He became an instructor at one of only two instrument schools set up by the Army Air Corps. One was at Lubbock Army Air Field, in Texas, where he was assigned.

He had one of the very first "green cards" as they were called, which meant he had no weather minimums for takeoff or landing and could sign his own flight clearance at any time.

At Lubbock, on the wind-swept high plains, the weather can be capricious and unpredictable. He was making a landing one day which could have ended his flying career, or at least put a blemish on his record. On final and almost to touchdown his aircraft experienced a sudden wind shift and what had been correct approach speed abruptly dropped precipitously. It was a very hard landing. When Buck reported what had happened it seemed too much for his commander to believe and the accident was about to be marked down as pilot error when the base Weather Officer reported that he had at that moment been watching the wind gauge and observed that incredible switch in direction of the strong wind.

He still had to have a check ride of course. He performed flawlessly and the instructor said, "Let's see a three point over the fence." Clearing the fence by mere feet he sat the AT-6 smoothly down on main gear and tail wheel. The check pilot said rather laconically, as Buck later put it, "I'm satisfied. Let's just sit here a while and watch others do their landings, and then we'll taxi in."

Buck had entered the army as a respected but relatively poor young man straight off the farm. He had proven his mettle in battle and in every way you could ask a young officer to prove himself. He was offered a prized opportunity, the chance to move to a unit formed to fly P-61 "Black Widows" in thunderstorm penetration to help advance research into the conditions inside those monsters of the Great Plains.

He would have been the ideal pilot for that duty. Top drawer instrument skills, demonstrated coolness under fire, and iron nerves. That high-profile assignment might well have been the stepping stone to further career advancement. However that duty apparently did not strike his wife as something she would put up with and, badly as he wanted it, he reluctantly turned down the assignment.

There is no doubt in my mind that he could have been a general officer had he remained in uniform. No, he had no degree, but with his academic ability, drive, and military programs for degree completion, that would have come. Certainly he would have been a splendid role model. You could pick him out in any group: slim and strong, he wore the uniform as if born to it.

He had an intense desire to remain on active duty, and, because he was one of a select early group of instrument instructors, I believe he could have. Unfortunately another problem surfaced. Years prior to their marriage, his wife had contracted rheumatic fever. As time went by, doctors they consulted told him that if he remained in uniform, subject to possible transfer to a station with a climate less favorable for her, she might experience life-threatening complications. Concerned for her welfare, he made a very difficult decision: to leave the Army Air Corps, pick a location recommended by the doctors for her continued health, and find a job there to support her.

He had found great fulfillment as an instructor pilot at Lubbock and his wife's doctors recommended that area, so West Texas seemed a natural choice for a location to move and look for a job.

Although an excellent self-taught carpenter, once out of uniform he was viewed as just one more demobilized soldier looking for work. After they pulled their trailer house to West Texas, he had gone to the State Employment Office to register for work where a man asked him, "Can you dig post holes?" He said, "Yes, and I need a job." He was hired by a Lubbock construction company and went to work as a laborer, digging post holes under the hot West Texas sun. Eventually, due to his native ability and hard work, he became a journeyman carpenter, then what he called a "straw boss", later a foreman, and then construction job boss. Before his career came to a close he had gained a proven reputation as one of the best construction superintendents in the West Texas area, building hospitals and shopping malls, and a variety of other jobs.

Always willing to do whatever he could for his family, soon after he located in Lubbock, a college town, he took our younger brother under his wing and let him sleep on his sofa in his 'trailer house' and later put a small room on the home he built himself, so his little brother could go to college. It was the kid's only chance. The farm in remote rural Nebraska, where he lived with his mother and step father (our father had been killed in a railroad accident) was far from any college and there was no money to live away from home and pay tuition. It was the kid's only opportunity and it changed his life for the better. His little brother's presence sometimes introduced strain into Buck's household but he was determined that the boy would have the chance he never had.

Robert was widely respected for his ability, his work ethic, and his integrity. His boys, one of whom later completed his university degree and became a construction superintendent himself, had early on become skilled carpenters. With company approval both were working on a job with a short deadline, where crews were working overtime. One Friday afternoon the firm's owner dropped into the main office and decided to look through the checks to be handed out that day. He looked at one son's check and then the other's. They had worked the same hours as the other rush crews but he unwisely chose that moment to make an insulting remark about the, "... Gaston boys making a lot of money that week." Buck properly took that as an insult to his integrity and quit on the spot.

Word quickly got around and before he arrived home the phone was ringing, and before nine o'clock he had a new job, as superintendent on a significant construction project just getting underway in Lubbock.

I knew him well and fully understood that bitter disappointment and a strong sense of lost opportunity marked his tough transition to civilian life, but he kept it to himself. An officer and a gentleman, a proven veteran of the war over Europe, and the possessor of an elite instrument rating suddenly became an unskilled laborer. I knew in my heart he wanted a service career and wanted it badly. But his sense of duty took him down a different road. On that road however he never lost his intensity or his concern for others. He was active in Red Cross safety training and supported his sons' and his wife's scouting activities where she was recognized with the rare "Silver Fawn" award.

Stricken with adult-onset diabetes (The result of stress? I have always thought so.) He rose early every morning, administered his insulin doses, fixed his own breakfast, and was on the job site early, without fail. He was a real man.

In spite of his strenuous activity and his strict, self-imposed diet, the disease finally took its toll. He was on the job when his eyesight suddenly began to worsen. He calmly climbed into his truck and drove to his home, realizing that it was now or never, and that he probably would never drive again. He has been gone now for a number of years, stricken by a heart attack likely brought on by his long term illness.

Brother Buck, I salute you. You were the ideal I always wanted to live up to. I'll see you again someday, and we will fly airplanes.

Appendix One:
Planes Flown by John L. Gaston

Piper J-3 Cub

Ryan PT-22

Vultee BT-13 Valiant

North American AT-6

Curtiss Rock AT-9

P-47

Douglas A-24

P-51

L-5

Aeronca

Interstate

Tailorcraft

Luscombe 8-A

B-25

AT-11

C-45

AT-7

DC-3/C-47

DC-4/C-54

B-17

C-124

Cessna 310

Cessna 140

Cessna 401

Cessna 4-2

Cessna 411

Cessna 421

Cessna 206

Cessna 150

Cessna 172

Piper Navajo

Piper Seneca

Beechcraft Baron

Beechcraft Turbo Charged Light Twin Duke

Piper Aztec

Piper Turbo Aztec

Beechcraft Queenair

Beechcraft Kingair C-90

MU-2

Sweringen Turbo Prop

Cessna Citation

Saberliner 60

Saberliner 60A

Saberliner 65

Falcon 50

Appendix Two: Pictures from the Dedication of the Monument to the Checkertails in Lesina, Italy, 2014

In October 2014 the citizens of Lesina, Italy, honored the brave young American men who fought in the skies over Europe to defeat Nazi forces and help ensure the freedom of the Italian people. It was a touching thing they did, and the few remaining men left of the 325th Fighter Group, their families, and their friends appreciated it more than words can tell.

Few traces of the fighter base near Lesina are left. But in the hearts of those who were children when the Americans were stationed nearby, and in the hearts of their children, memories remain. A lady came up me, the only pilot able to attend, and told of a time, when she was a child, and ill, with no doctor available. Her mother took her to the Checkertail base, and the flight surgeon took time from his duties to treat the little girl and give her mother medicine which she took home.

Those of us who are left, our families, and all the members of the Checkertail Clan organization will cherish our memories of the warmth and regard of the people of Lesina. We came as strangers and now feel we are family. Thank you.

OFFICINA FORTE
MECCANICA
ELETTRAUTO
GOMMISTA
WELCOME BACK, HEROES!

VIVISPORT

ALBERGO
BAR
WELCOME BACK, HEROES!

P-47
CONSILIUM CONFICTUR
P-51
325th FIGHTER GROUP
317th, 318th, 319th FIGHTER SQUADRONS
WORLD WAR II
U.S. ARMY AIR FORCE
MEDITERRANEAN THEATER
LESINA MARCH 29, 1944 TO MARCH 2, 1945
HONORING ALL WHO SERVED
DEDICATED MAY 16, 2014
LESINA, ITALY
15

P-47
P-51
325th FIGHTER GROUP
317th, 318th, 319th FIGHTER SQUADRONS
WORLD WAR II
U.S. ARMY AIR FORCE
MEDITERRANEAN THEATER
LESINA MARCH 29, 1944 TO MARCH 2, 1945
HONORING ALL WHO SERVED
DEDICATED MAY 16, 2014
LESINA, ITALY
15

325th FIGHTER GROUP

325th FIGHTER GROUP
WORLD WAR II
U.S. ARMY AIR FORCE
MEDITERRANEAN THEATER

325th FIGHTER GROUP
WORLD WAR II
U.S. ARMY AIR FORCE
MEDITERRANEAN THEATER

Biographies of the Authors

John Gaston enlisted in the U.S. Army Aviation Cadet program, fresh out of high school in 1942, when he turned eighteen. He completed the rigorous program of flight training for aviation cadets and received his silver wings at the age of nineteen. He celebrated his twentieth birthday in the middle of the Atlantic Ocean on an LST bound for the European Theater of War. Once at sea his small group of new pilots discovered they had no official orders. Disembarking in North Africa they made their way to Italy where they walked into the headquarters of the 325th Fighter Group, the Checkertail Clan, unexpected but badly needed replacement pilots. He served with distinction as a member of the Checkertail Clan, earning the Distinguished Flying Cross and the Air Medal with several Oak Leaf Clusters. His memories of those days, and of the men he served with, are among his proudest.

Following the war he served in the Army Air Corps and the Air Force as a Master Sergeant, completing weather school, and serving as a weather forecaster.

Recalled to active duty as an officer he held a number of responsible positions, but he always longed for an assignment with flying as his primary duty. He achieved that goal when he flew with the 85th Air Transport Squadron, flying missions over the Pacific, some under hazardous conditions, as Aircraft Commander in the C-124. Major Gaston served as Meteorlogist and Staff Briefer at NORAD and he retired as a Lieutenant Colonel in 1965.

Building on his experience and training he then had a successful fifteen year career as a corporate pilot, flying the most modern executive aircraft, including - upon its debut - his favorite, the Falcon 50.

Dr. Gaston entered the Air Force as a Second Lieutenant and was immediately assigned to one of the laboratories in the Wright Field complex. He completed a thirty year career in the Research and Development field with active duty assignments at Wright Patterson, and reserve assignments with Hq. USAF, Hq. Air Force Systems Command, and the Department of Aerospace Studies at the Weapons Lab at Kirtland AFB. He retired in 1986 in the grade of Colonel.